"The selling process that we have established based on *The Six Steps to Excellence in Selling* has helped us increase our customer base and year to date sales by 20%. This system is the most effective way I have found to grow my business."

Dave Nebel, Owner, Eden Prairie Florist

"Finally, a sales book with a marketing perspective. Anyone who sells should read this book."

John Hunt, Bright Marketing

"We were floundering. Warren and his "Six Steps" helped us get our sales effort on track with the right prospects, people, techniques and attitude. We no longer wasted valuable time and resources calling on the wrong people. The "Six Steps" are now a key part of our business plan. To say the least, this is an important part of my business - you not only need good products or services, you need a good "front lines" plan to develop your client base!"

Bob Pigozzi, Vice President, Marketing, Archco, Inc., Fuel Management Specialists

"My progress in my selling career was accelerated by years because of Mr. Wechsler's selling program. I am much further ahead than I would have been had I tried to learn all these skills on my own.

Paul Gonyea, Gonyea Commercial Properties

THE SIX STEPS TO EXCELLENCE IN SELLING

The Step-by-Step Guide to Effective Selling

by

Warren Wechsler

The Six Steps to Excellence in Selling—
The step-by-step guide to effective selling

Editor Kristine E. Ellis

Wechsler, Warren M., 1953 -

The Six Steps to Excellence in Selling: The step-by-step guide to effective selling/Warren Wechsler

p. cm.

Includes bibliographical references and index.

ISBN 1-886656-06-1

Library of Congress Catalog
Card Number: 94-96734

1. Selling	2. Sales	
3. Sales management	4. Small business	
5. Self help	6. Marketing	I. Title

Printed and bound in the United States of America

99 98 97 96 95 10 9 8 7 6 5 4 3 2 1

THE SIX STEPS TO EXCELLENCE IN SELLING

TABLE OF CONTENTS

ACKNOWLEDGEMENTS

So many ideas and so much support and encouragement were given to me by so many people. This book would not have become a reality without them. To all of them, I offer thanks:

To the late Richard Nelson, who introduced me to the ideals of "the profession" of selling.

To Tom Hopkins, who empowered and encouraged me over the years to be the best sales trainer I can be.

To Chuck Watson, Debby Magnuson, Tina Healy and Jay Abdo, who read my manuscript and gave me feedback, suggestions, and new ways of looking at my concepts.

To Jody Majeres, who brought my vision to life with color, design and visual clarity.

To Kristine Ellis, who edited and proofed the words.

To Kristine Anderson, who put it all together for me.

To Bob Pearl, who caught my enthusiasm for selling on film.

To John Hunt, who met with me weekly and helped me chart my progress.

To John Hey, who allowed me to develop and use my ideas while I was a sales manager for him.

To my clients, who proved the validity of my selling concepts by using them to increase their own selling effectiveness.

To Sam Wechsler, my late father, who was a salesperson all his life, and inspired me through my memories.

To Frieda Rosenberg, my mother, who always clipped articles and gave me new ideas.

To Jack Rosenberg, my stepfather, who always reminded me that I had something valid to say.

To my two daughters, Alison and Bhavani, who love me unconditionally and always think I am wonderful, even when I doubt myself.

And finally, to my wife, Gail Young, who believed in me, encouraged me, never gave up on me, supported me, listened to me, kept me going and showed me by living her own life each and every day how to have values, courage, and persistence — the attributes that made it possible for me to complete this book.

Why This Book Is Different

If you're like many salespeople, you've read books, listened to tapes and attended seminars on selling, motivation and personal development. Maybe you've even thought, "Why can't I find a book that's easy to read, easy to understand, easy to apply? A how-to manual filled with practical ideas presented in self-contained chapters. A book that can be read in one sitting! One that's easy to refer to when I need a quick refresher or some insight into my own selling career. I don't need another book filled with jargon, manipulation tactics and outdated concepts."

This is the book you've been looking for. *The Six Steps to Excellence in Selling* combines the whys, whats and hows of selling in one book. It is simple to understand. It is based on common sense. It teaches the sales process in six concise steps that are easy to learn and apply.

And virtually anyone can use the ideas presented in these pages.

This book gives you a blueprint for success — a living, tangible plan that will help you reach your personal, professional and career objectives while you're providing your clients with the highest level of value — virtually guaranteeing you ongoing success and fulfillment.

WHY "GO GET 'EM!" DOESN'T WORK

Every year one out of every three salespeople either fails to reach their selling goals or quits their company or chosen field. Others do okay but never reach their full potential. In my opinion most of these people fail because they have never been taught the "profession of selling." If they had become doctors, lawyers, architects or engineers, they would have spent years in academia studying the principles of their field. They would have learned from experienced mentors, had the best textbooks and benefitted from the successful experiences of those who had entered the field before them.

In my own early selling career, and in the early careers of others whom I know, people who came to selling from backgrounds in marketing, economics, engineering and the like, there is a rather common and unfortunate bond. None of us had any formal education in the principles of selling. We all were similarly prepared (or unprepared) for our careers. We were handed a catalog of company information, a telephone and a phone book and told by our sales manager or the owner of the company to "go get 'em." Perhaps many of you had a boss who was an "instructor" or a "graduate" of the Go Get 'Em School.

Imagine what would have happen if, having decided to become a brain surgeon instead of a salesperson, you were handed a scalpel on the first day of medical school, pointed toward the operating room where a patient was waiting and told by the chief surgeon to "go get 'em." Imagine if the contractor building your dream home handed a hammer to a new employee with no experience, gave him some wood and said "go get 'em." Imagine if the law firm representing you gave your file to a first-year law student, pointed her in the direction of the courtroom and said "go get 'em."

Ludicrous, isn't it? Yet many of us are put into situations like this every day because no one ever gave us the tools or taught us the techniques necessary to be successful in a selling environment.

My manager told me, "You have a great attitude and your test results show that you have the right blend of abilities to be successful. Our company has an excellent reputation and a wonderful mix of products. Our service is second to none. Your territory is the major metropolitan area, and your catalog is at your desk, along with your phone and a box of business cards. I know you'll be great. Now GO GET 'EM!"

It didn't work for me. It doesn't work for most people. I was initially a failure in my selling career. I soon realized that my positive attitude, product knowledge, hard work and company support were only part of the story. I had to learn how to be an effective and successful salesperson. So I began the process of learning everything that I could about the selling business. I talked to successful salespeople and found that some people who are excellent at selling are not always good at conveying and teaching the hows and whys of their success to other people. I read many books, listened to lots of tapes and attended numerous seminars on the topics of selling, motivation, goal setting and time management. They were helpful.

As I began to understand the basic principles of selling, my sales began to increase. In fact, they doubled in one year. And as my sales grew, my confidence grew. My success soon led to promotions, and I found myself in sales management positions where I had the opportunity to help others get off on the right foot in their selling careers. Remembering my own successes and failures, I thought that the best way to share my knowledge would be to suggest to others that they read books, attend seminars and listen to audio cassettes on the topics of selling, motivation, goal setting and time management — just like I had. But as I thought about it, I realized that I had spent years picking up ideas from numerous sources. Some of the information I had absorbed focused on motivation, some on principles of selling, some on attitude, some on goal setting and some on a wide array of other topics.

But not one book, tape or seminar told me the whole story.

No one source explained the principles of selling and offered the practical, hands-on, here's-how-you-do-it knowledge that I developed on my own. Throughout my sales career, by studying classical sales theory and observing the techniques of top salespeople, I learned what works best. But not until I became a manager and began working with and training other salespeople did I realize that I could not point to one organized system of knowledge and say to a new salesperson, here are the principles, here is what you need to do, and here is how to do it.

So I decided to create a blueprint for selling success by writing down the principles I had learned, used and developed. I knew that in any field of endeavor a step-by-step approach built on a strong foundation yields the best results and that the go get 'em model was not going to cut it. I also knew that a program based on activities had always worked best for me and the people I managed. I decided that the best model for my blueprint would be one that was simple to understand, easy to follow and based on common sense.

The result is my six-step blueprint for the profession of selling. It's practical, professional and nonmanipulative, and it is my pleasure and honor to share with you. It offers an organized, easy-to-follow, step-by-step approach that enables salespeople and other business and professional people to achieve success and fulfill their potential in selling.

That's why this book is different.

WHY THIS BOOK CAN BE IMPORTANT TO YOU

You may be like me, self-taught and initially exposed to the go get 'em model. You may be searching for a one-stop source that affirms what you are doing well and answers questions about how to improve or overcome weaknesses in your selling efforts.

Or maybe you are new to sales and looking for a source that

can teach you the whys, whats and hows in a nonmanipulative and empowering manner.

Maybe you're an entrepreneur or business owner who is looking for a holistic and honest way to begin and maintain a marketing program for your business.

Maybe you're a manager or marketing professional who works with and through salespeople, and you're wondering what this business of selling is all about and if salespeople are better than the sometimes unflattering stereotypes people carry around. (Yes, a lot better!)

Maybe you are a seasoned sales professional who is looking for a way to enhance and refresh your skills.

If any of these people sound like you, or if you are looking for a simple, complete and honest step-by-step approach to the profession of selling, then this book is what you need. All of the ideas, techniques, approaches, plans and proven methods that I have shared with thousands of people in my public and corporate programs are written down for you in this book.

THE SIX STEPS

Why are there six steps to the selling process? Why not four or seven or sixteen? Those are good questions, and I am asked them quite often during my seminars. (No, I was not struck by lightning one day resulting in a brilliant flash of insight. Neither was I awakened from a deep sleep and given the magic secret by the ghost of some long-deceased, superlative salesperson.)

By watching my own career and those of other successful salespeople, I saw that there was a system to selling just like there is a system to building a home or learning how to swim. As a sales manager, I worked with many salespeople in the field. After traveling with them, and usually over dinner or lunch, I would invariably take out a piece of paper, or make use of a napkin or placemat, and begin to counsel them as to where they needed work. Over and over I found myself drawing a pyramid with six levels and pointing out where they were strong, where they were weak and what they could focus on to improve.

Once I identified the six distinct steps, I found that my own sales and the sales of the people I managed increased by simply making sure that these simple steps were understood and followed. Identifying the six steps gave us a common language and a blueprint by which we could measure ourselves to make sure we were on track.

I discovered another great benefit of this step-by-step model when I used it to analyze a loss of momentum or sales. I could simply refer to the well-defined model to see what specific improvements or changes had to be made. Soon after adjustments were made, sales increased. This worked equally on the macro level (territory) and on the micro level (particular account).

The Six Steps

STEP ONE is Find the Prospect. A prospect is defined as a potential client who is likely to have a need for our products or services. For instance, say you are in the jet airplane business. Are you going to go to the local gas station to try and sell a corporate jet? Probably not. Typically, local gas stations are not your best prospects for multimillion dollar airplanes. There are good and bad prospects for any business or salesperson, and an understanding of who the best prospects are and how to find them is critical to excellent sales performance. So the first thing we have to learn is the best way to go about finding the right people to talk to about our products and services.

STEP TWO is Find the Decision Maker. How many times have you discovered, far into your discussions with a company you've identified as a good prospect, that you are talking to the wrong person? You find out that the president of the company makes all buying decisions, and you've spent your time doing a needs analysis, presentation and proposal for the office manager. Or maybe it's a branch office; you learn the decision is made in Chicago, but your territory is Minneapolis. The point is, you need to do some digging for information about your prospect before you make the initial selling approach.

√ **STEP THREE is Arrange an Appointment.** Before we can become actively involved in the "selling" phase of our business, we have to be face to face (or phone to phone, in the case of telephone-oriented sales) with the people with whom we might develop a business relationship. In our zeal and enthusiasm to accomplish this we sometimes might get on the phone and just push people into seeing us. Have you ever been approached this way, either in your business or at home? Remember when someone was overly aggressive or even borderline unethical in pursuit of an appointment with you? How did you feel?

These manipulative, aggressive strategies are often unsuccessful, not to mention unprofessional. People slam down the phone or ask us to leave their reception area. It's very unpleasant. And it's unnecessary. There are positive things we can do to arrange appointments. There are some very effective opening statements we can use that will lead to or result in the potential prospect saying, "Sure, come on in, let's talk", without any further questions or an examination. There are creative, attention-getting approaches that will produce well-intentioned, well-positioned appointments. There are nonmanipulative techniques that will help us overcome the reflex resistance that we often face as salespeople.

? **STEP FOUR is Ask Questions and Listen.** After we set the appointment, our excitement builds. We have a prospect. We know who the decision maker is, and we have an appointment. Unfortunately, this is a point in the selling process where many salespeople go astray. Because of our excitement and our comfort level with speaking about our products, our services and our company, we may have a tendency to start telling our story too soon, before we've earned the right to do so.

Imagine you've been given the privilege of an appointment with the decision maker of a very, very good prospect for your products. Do you start off the conversation by telling her how great your products are, before asking questions about her company's situation? This would be like a doctor scheduling you for a heart transplant before he examined you or even asked you any questions. Would you want to work with that doctor? Of course not. Like a good doctor, a good salesperson needs to spend time asking the right questions. Our goal in Step Four is to probe for information about the decision maker's goals, the company, the current situation, unmet needs and the like, and then attentively listen to the answers.

! **STEP FIVE is Present the Solution.** This is the point in the sales process where we share those exciting stories with the prospect about how many years we've been in business and why that experience may be important. We may even present a list of satisfied clients or a testimonial letter that we've received from someone in a business similar to theirs. We might say, here is some information about my company, here's a corporate brochure that explains our services, and finally, here's the product that I recommend based on my analysis of your explanation of your situation. Everything is moving along well during Step Five, and the stage is now set for the successful completion of the business transaction and the beginning of the client/salesperson relationship.

$ **STEP SIX is Ask for the Commitment.** As odd as it may seem, many potential sales are lost because salespeople do not come right out and ask the prospective customer for the business. Many salespeople think that closing the sale is the hardest part of the sales process. But it is only a small, though important, part of the big picture, and it is really quite simple. Understanding how people arrive at decisions and why they might not be as willing to move forward is important knowledge and gives us key insights into how to help people become involved with our products and services.

THE SIX-STEP PYRAMID

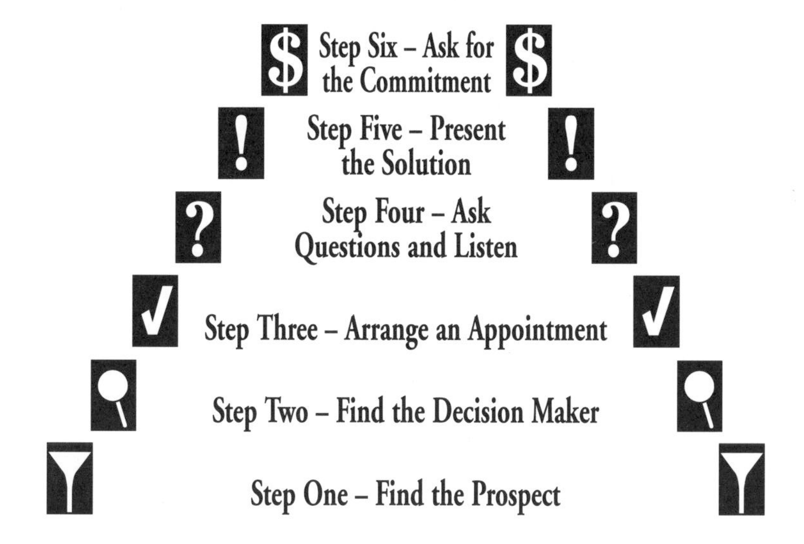

Envision the selling process as a pyramid with six steps. As with a pyramid, building a successful sales business begins with building a firm foundation. The structure cannot stand nor rise above ground without it. In selling, this broad base is Step One. Finding the prospect is like laying the foundation.

Building on the strong support of Step One, we move on to Step Two and find the decision maker. This step is similar to the work done by famous detectives, such as Sherlock Holmes. Just like Holmes, we look for clues — ideas, names and facts that will help us solve our mystery.

Once the detective work is completed, it is time for direct contact with the people with whom we want to do business.

Step Three, arrange an appointment, continues to build on the knowledge and information gained in Steps One and Two, opening the door for us to share our ideas and information with our prospects. Step Four, ask questions and listen, is the chance to be the sales consultant, letting the prospect share their needs, desires, fears and motivations. We focus on actively observing and listening. Then, after we learn what the prospect is looking for, we can present the solution, Step Five. This is our opportunity to take center stage and enthusiastically present our ideas on how we can deliver the answers our prospect needs. Finally, we move the process to its natural conclusion with Step Six, when we ask for the commitment and the prospect becomes a customer.

In the chapters that follow, we'll look at the six steps in great detail. You will gain an understanding of the concepts and learn specific ways to apply the steps and personalize them for your own business, industry and company.

Let's get started!

The First Step–Find the Prospect

Every journey begins with a first step. Step One, Find the Prospect, is a lot like farming. Before harvesting the bumper crop, the farmer decides what to plant, then buys the seeds, prepares the ground, plants the seeds, waters the fields, remove the weeds, nurtures the plants and finally, many weeks or months later, harvests the crop. Prospecting is equivalent to preparing our own fertile selling ground, planting our seeds of future clients, watering and nurturing the best prospects and weeding out the ones not worthy of pursuit.

I cannot emphasize the importance of this first step too strongly. At the base of our sales pyramid, we're laying the foundation for our selling success when we determine the types and numbers of our current, future and potential clients.

One salesperson's story will illustrate the critical importance of prospecting. Bill, a mortgage banker in a large midwestern city, learned through the business section of his daily newspaper (a prospecting resource that will be discussed later in this chapter) that a large out-of-town company intended to acquire a retailer based in his city. There are more than 250 mortgage bankers in this particular city, and how many do you think saw the opportunity and made a long-distance call? Amazingly enough, Bill was the only one. After many months of follow up and hard work, Bill's initial phone call ultimately led to the completion of a $49 million mortgage and a six-figure commission.

Deciding whom to call on, where to find them and how to organize the information is arguably the most important activity that any professional salesperson does.

DEFINITION OF A PROSPECT

A prospect is a person, company or organization with whom we would like to develop a business relationship. Those we define as prospects come from our own research, which helps us predetermine who the top prospects should be. The prospect is not necessarily interested in doing business with us and may not even know that we exist. At this stage of the process, we don't know if the people or companies we've identified as potential prospects are good prospects. That's okay. Later in the process we'll have a chance to test our assumptions.

FILLING THE PIPELINE

Selling can also be viewed as a funnel leading into a pipeline. In a funnel, the wide top tapers to a narrow cylinder. A lot of water needs to be poured into the top for a steady stream to flow out the end. Similarly, in the sales process, we need to keep putting lots of prospects into our sales funnel to have customers, sales and money flowing through our business pipeline. If we don't have a constant source of numerous new prospects, our sales businesses will be merely a trickle.

WHY DON'T SALESPEOPLE PROSPECT?

If prospecting is so important (and it is!), why don't some of us want to do it? In my experience, there are three reasons: lack of prospecting skills, lack of time and fear of rejection. Let's look at them individually and see how to overcome each obstacle to prospecting.

Lack of prospecting skills

Many of us lack the skills to develop a comprehensive plan for our sales business because our background is the go get 'em model. Finding sources for prospects, knowing how to organize prospect information and other prospecting knowledge has not been readily available to us. Some of us were given extensive technical training in our chosen field and have lots of product knowledge, yet we were not formally introduced to effective prospecting ideas. So in this step we'll learn prospecting skills and develop a prospecting plan.

Lack of time to prospect

Lack of time is the second reason that people don't prospect. This obstacle is a function of what I call the "Theory of Too." I have always believed that there are only "too" reasons that we don't have the time to prospect.

- It's too early.
- It's too late.
- It's too hot.
- It's too cold.
- It's too nice outside.
- It's too hard.
- It's too slow.
- I'm too busy.
- I'm too tired.

Do you get the picture?

Too reasons are more often problems with time management and incorrect perceptions of prospecting than valid reasons for not prospecting. For example, the common wisdom has always been that salespeople should not conduct prospecting activities on Monday mornings or Friday afternoons. But, in reality, these are often the best times to contact high-level people. The weather does not affect prospecting success either. In fact, rainy and cold days find more people available than do very hot days. The busier you are, the more important prospecting becomes so that your sales funnel receives a steady stream of fresh input. If you're not busy, prospecting becomes even more important.

The way to overcome the obstacle of "too" is to schedule your prospecting activities just like you schedule your appointments. In this case, you are making an appointment with yourself to conduct your prospecting. It's an application of the principle of *scheduled activities drive out unscheduled activities*, also known as time blocking. We schedule, or block out, times of the day or week to prospect just as we do for appointments, meetings, personal activities and the like. In my experience, prospecting is the easiest activity to forget or put off doing. It takes a lot of energy, is filled with potential rejection and is interruptive by nature. So the only way to ensure that it happens on a regular basis is to block out the time and do it.

Fear of rejection

Fear of rejection is the third reason people don't prospect. It is one of the major obstacles to success in selling. Many salespeople let fear defeat them before they even begin. They fill their minds with all of the reasons people will be rude, mean, busy or uninterested.

There is another way of looking at this. In fact, let's take the fear to its extreme. What is the worst thing that could possibly happen on an initial call? Can those you call send poison darts through the phone lines? Can they physically harm you? Can they take away your profession? Of course they can't. But many people have an unrealistic fear of calling people for the first time. It is true that the prospect might be busy, in an important meeting, not mentally prepared to hear your initial message or even not interested. It is also true that you are proactively interrupting the prospect at some level. But what really is the worst thing that could happen?

Take a few minutes and write out your response. Get your fears out in the open.

I think you'll find that the worst thing that could happen is that the prospect says no or is rude to you. If so, because you have "too many prospects," a concept that will be explained later, you simply shrug your shoulders, momentarily mourn this loss and then move on to the next call. It's not so bad after all.

Becoming neutral to the outcome

Another way of handling fear of rejection is to train ourselves to become neutral to the outcome of every sales activity. This does not mean that we are neutral about our company, products and services, or that we are indifferent to whether the prospect will do business with us. Rather, this concept teaches us that while we can control our own activities, like our initial calls, what we're going to say and the like, we cannot control the outcome of our activities.

We always give our best effort, presuming that we'll be able to be of service to a particular prospect. If they are open to our initial approach, then that's great! If not, we'll move on to the next prospect. We don't let each individual rejection set us back because we know that eventually someone will be open. We just don't know which prospect it will be — the next one or the next one after that or the next one after that. We'll look at remaining neutral to the outcome more in Step Six.

WHY SALESPEOPLE MUST PROSPECT

The sale cannot be completed until it is started, and prospecting is the beginning of the entire process. Because people are not generally beating a path to our door, it is up to us to make the first move. Let's look at prospecting in another way:

- Prospecting leads us to potential customers.
- A certain number of potential customers become satisfied clients.
- Satisfied clients generate income for the salesperson.
- Income makes salespeople happy and feeling successful.
- Successful and happy salespeople have high self-esteem.
- High self-esteem makes salespeople willing to talk to lots of people.
- Wanting to talk to lots of people leads to prospecting activities.
- And the cycle begins anew.

THE RIGHT NUMBER OF PROSPECTS

How many prospects do we need? The exact number varies for different businesses. But no matter what, there are only three quantities of prospects that a salesperson could possibly have. The choices are:

- Exactly enough prospects
- Too many prospects
- Not enough prospects

Exactly enough prospects would mean that at the end of a given sales period, whether weekly, monthly or annually, you would contact the last person on your list of prospects and that person would decide to get involved in your product or service, thus ensuring that you reached the goal you had set for yourself. In all my years of selling, I have never met anyone who had exactly enough prospects.

Too many prospects does not mean that we have so many prospects that we feel overwhelmed or unable to organize the huge list. It means that we think we have more people to call on than we can handle on a given day. In this situation, when a particular prospect rejects us, we shrug our shoulders, evaluate the experience to see if there was anything we did wrong or could do better the next time and then move on to the next contact armed with the knowledge that because we have "too many" prospects, there are still plenty more people to contact. Even with the rejection, we are able to reach our realistic and challenging sales goal at the end of the sales period. We always want to have too many prospects.

This leaves us with the third option, **not enough prospects.** Most salespeople often find themselves in this situation during their selling career. The tragedy is that these people usually blame the lack of success that accompanies this problem on somebody or something else. When I work with salespeople on improving their performance, nine times out of ten the area needing the most work is increasing the number of prospects in the pipeline.

Why is this so important? Imagine that you have a sales goal of completing ten transactions in the month of June. You know that you usually do business with 50% of the people to whom you present your solutions. With four days left in the month, you find that you have completed six transactions. Of your appointments scheduled for the remaining days, you have meetings with only four prospects that are far enough along in the sales process to even considering asking for a commitment. You'll need to have commitments from four out of four! Pretty tough odds. In fact, you may feel so much on edge that you begin to press these last four people for commitments in an inappropriate way.

Now imagine that with four days left in the month you find that you have completed six transactions and have twelve more prospects that are far enough along in the sales process to ask for a commitment. Knowing that you usually do business with 50%

of those to whom you present solutions, you will exude a confidence that will enable the prospect to feel comfortable saying yes. And do you think that you could hear a final no from one of these twelve people and move on confidently to the next appointment without feeling defeated? I'll bet you would.

How many prospects are right for you? If you are selling corporate jets or multimillion dollar real estate properties, 100 prospects would be a lot. If you are selling insurance or carpet cleaning services, 1,000 might not be enough. As you analyze your own performance, perhaps you can see that to earn a particular dollar amount, you need to have a certain quantity of clients. Based on a closing ratio of 50%, you would need a certain number of appointments, and so on. You can develop a target number of prospects for yourself based on your own experiences, skills and ratios.

UNDERSTANDING SALES RATIOS

An understanding of the sales ratios in your business will help you determine the right number of prospects for you. Beginning with how much income you want, you can predict how many prospects you will need. In my selling career, I knew that if I contacted seven people per day in commercial real estate, I would attain my goals. In my consulting and training business, the number of contacts I need is two per day. In investment sales, the number of contacts is as high as twenty-five to thirty per day. Using the table on the next page, you can estimate the number you will need. Over time, by tracking your progress, you'll become more precise.

A STRATEGIC VIEW OF PROSPECTING

Step One is of critical strategic importance. Like building a home, if you start with a weak foundation, you're likely to have a home with a leaky basement, cracked walls and slanted floors. To ensure that we set ourselves up for the greatest chance of success

Estimated Number of Contacts Needed

Income desired (annual)	______________
Divided by average dollar volume per transaction	÷______________
Equals number of transactions	=______________
Divided by closing rate (if 50% use .50, 33% .33, etc.)	______________
Equals number of presentations needed	______________
Divided by appointments leading to presentations rate	÷______________
Equals number of appointments needed	=______________
Divided by prospecting calls leading to appointments rate	÷______________
Equals number of prospecting calls needed	=______________
Divided by weeks per year (use 50)	÷______________
Equals number of prospecting calls needed per peek	=______________
Divided by days per week (use 5)	÷______________
Equals number of prospecting calls needed per day	=______________

and the least likelihood of failure, we need to have a focused, sound and valid strategy for our prospecting efforts.

Prospecting matrix

The best prospects for a particular type of salesperson or industry are easier to identify than you might think. The key is to look at this first step in the selling process as a "strategic prospecting" approach. The following prospecting matrix will help you focus on the need for thinking strategically:

		PRODUCTS	
		(OLD) Current	(NEW) Potential/Future
PEOPLE	(OLD) Current Clients	1	2
	(NEW) Prospects	3	4

In order of ease of selling and effectiveness in approach (presuming that there is an established base of clients), quadrant one is the easiest and most effective, and quadrant four is the hardest and often least efficient manner of prospecting. Here's why. People buy from people they like and trust. It follows that people who know us and what we offer would be the easiest with which to develop additional business. Conversely, people we don't know and who have not purchased the particular item we're selling would be the most skeptical and offer the most resistance.

The easiest way to build our sales career is to offer more of what we provide to the people who already buy from us. The second easiest strategy is to offer new products or services to those same people. Third is to offer our current products and services to new people, and the most difficult strategy is to offer new product and service offerings to people with whom we have no relationship.

So **quadrant 1**, current products to current clients, is the easiest way to increase business. We simply go back to our current clients and offer more of the same product or service that they purchased from us in the past. (This sounds a lot easier than it is.) Many times in selling we become so excited about pursuing new business and talking about new ideas or new products and services that we forget that the people who are our lifeblood are our current clients.

Quadrant 2, new products to current clients, is the second best strategy to increase sales, offering new ideas, products and services to our current clients. After all, they already like and trust us and should be familiar with how well we perform, so they are the natural people to introduce to new alternatives. Current clients are the only source we have for cross-selling and the best place to introduce new ideas, products and services.

Quadrant 3, current products to new people (prospects), is a third strategy that a salesperson would likely pursue. In this scenario, we are offering potential clients a product or service known to benefit current clients. We are familiar with the benefits of the offering and the reasons why it would benefit potential users. This is a natural prospecting direction for a professional salesperson to pursue.

Quadrant 4, new products to new people, is the most difficult strategy to pursue. Imagine approaching someone you've never met and saying, "You've never met me, and this is a product that we've just starting offering to people like you. Do you want some?" This strategy is reserved for the trailblazing, pioneering, innovation-oriented company or salesperson. It's not easy, but under the right set of circumstances, such as coming into a new territory or introducing a new product line to a new market (and often out of necessity), it can be rewarding.

DEVELOPING A CAMPAIGN MENTALITY TOWARD PROSPECTING

It is the goal of all salespeople to increase their sales to the point where they are successful, highly motivated and happy with their own performance. With this in mind, many salespeople become single-minded and overly focused in the pursuit of one type of prospect. Prospecting that is too narrowly defined can lead to problems. When a narrow prospecting strategy is flawed, the salesperson can be setting him- or herself up for failure.

Let me give you a personal example. Many years ago, two successful target groups for my training seminars were the commercial printing and pre-press (color separation) industries. When I did an analysis of my prospect base, I decided to pursue advertising agencies. They were related to printing, and I knew that some of my printing and pre-press relationships could lead to referrals to some of the agencies. Despite my planning and strategizing, this turned out to be a flawed decision. The ad agencies at that point were not proactive. They did not see themselves as salespeople in need of training. In fact, they waited for clients and prospects to come to them when an advertising account came up for review or bid.

If I had limited my prospecting efforts to ad agencies exclusively for three months, I would have been in big trouble. At the end of that period, I would have had no new clients, an empty pipeline and a very low balance in my checkbook. It is very important, therefore, to develop our prospecting strategy as a blend of prospecting types and then pursue three to eight targeted prospecting campaigns concurrently. When we do this, we increase our chances of sales success and reduce our dependence on one industry or type of prospect.

Putting a campaign mentality to use

Once we determine what our sales goals are and what type of business and client base we want to establish, we simply need to select the number of campaigns we want to have ongoing. Three is a minimum (in case our logic is flawed on a particular campaign and it turns out not to be effective) and eight is a maximum (so we don't let our energy get too diffused). Examples of these campaigns are listed below. (The specifics are explained later in the chapter.)

- Who Do You Know Campaign
- Centers of Influence Campaign
- Current Client Contact Campaign
- Referral Campaign
- Geographic Prospecting Campaign
- Targeted Prospect Campaign Based on Selected Industries
- Targeted Prospect Campaign Based on Selected Directories or Resources
- Targeted Prospect Campaign Based on Selected Demographics
- Drive Around My Territory with a Dictaphone Campaign

As you read over the following information be thinking about which campaigns you want to include in your prospecting efforts.

SOURCES OF PROSPECTS

There are virtually unlimited sources of prospects. Once you establish your list of target prospects and the quantity that you need, it is simply a matter of looking over the following source material and choosing the best options for you. Some of the sources listed will be better for industrial or commercial sales, and others will be better for consumer or personal services selling. Some resources will work only if you have or work with an established business, and others will work better if you are starting from scratch. Any one of these sources can be turned into a prospecting campaign.

It really is who you know

One interesting way to use your past experiences and contacts as a way to build a prospecting campaign is to ask yourself the question, "Who do I know because of my..." and then list some categories. Once you have some names in place, you then call these people and ask them if they know anyone who falls into any of your target prospecting categories. For example, who do you know because of your:

- Schooling
- Family
- Previous job(s)
- Hobbies
- Community activities
- Church or synagogue
- Home ownership or rental
- Neighborhood
- Automobile
- Personal grooming

Five people from each category equals fifty potential contacts. Ten people from each category equals 100 potential contacts.

Centers of influence

Closely related to the who-do-you-know prospecting approach is identifying and contacting centers of influence in your geographic area. These are bankers, accountants, lawyers, business leaders, community leaders, religious leaders and other influential people. Depending on your product or service, a call to a well-connected center of influence can open doors and plant the seed for future referral and networking opportunities.

Analysis of current clients

We need to analyze our current clients to determine if there is a common theme or type of person with whom we have been the most successful. We're looking for patterns of industry, demographics, source of business and so on. Here's an easy way to do this. Take out a sheet of paper and write down the following:

My 10 Best Clients

(in terms of revenues, loyalty, profit, referrals, etc.)

WHO WHERE DID THEY COME FROM

1. ______________________________
2. ______________________________
3. ______________________________
4. ______________________________
5. ______________________________
6. ______________________________
7. ______________________________
8. ______________________________
9. ______________________________
10. ______________________________

Now fill in the blanks. If you are brand new to selling or to the company or industry you're now representing, you'll have to talk to more experienced people or your management to complete this exercise. It's important to do this. Knowing where these people came from will help you determine where to go to find more just like them.

Dream prospects and nontraditional uses of your products

Have you ever thought to yourself, "I really think that _______________ (industry, company, person, geographic area) would benefit from my product or service," and then not taken the time to look into it? Have you considered nontraditional or emerging uses of your products or services? Take some time now to identify these.

My 10 Best Dream Prospects

(industry, company, person, geographic area)

WHO WHERE MIGHT THEY COME FROM

1. ____
2. ____
3. ____
4. ____
5. ____
6. ____
7. ____
8. ____
9. ____
10. ____

These two lists can help you begin to develop another campaign approach to your prospecting efforts. As you review your two lists, look for similarities or identifying characteristics. Are the companies large or small, local or national, proprietorships or corporations, entrepreneurial or professionally managed, geographically concentrated or diverse? Are the people old or young, experienced or inexperienced, sophisticated or simple, male or female, friendly or purely businesslike? Are there any trends that you can see?

Using these two lists, come up with several types of prospects that you want to target. It can be as general as "dry cleaners" or as specific as "dry cleaners with multiple locations on the east side of Chicago." The major point is to identify the people and companies who are going to be privileged to be in your prospecting universe and then build a base of prospects that will enable you to reach your goals. Then create a campaign.

Current customer files

Current customer files (if you have current clients) are usually the first place to look for prospects. There are two reasons why our current and satisfied clients are the *best* source of new business. First, they can buy ongoing and additional products or services from us. Second, your search of your files can result in new product applications and referral business.

In Step Four, we will discuss in great detail how people buy from people who they like and trust. But right now, consider this. Who likes you and trusts you more than someone or some company who is already doing business with you? Our prospecting matrix tells us that the easiest way to build market share and sales is to offer more of what you have to people who already buy from you. Before I started my sales training, consulting and seminar business, I was involved in office equipment sales and then commercial real estate. There were clients who bought office equipment from me, then asked me to help them with their commercial real estate needs and then actually helped me launch my consulting business by becoming my first clients. Recalling the prospecting matrix, you will see that I applied the principle from quadrant two — offering new ideas and services to past or current clients.

Some salespeople think that they call on their current clients too much and that they are pests. Studies and my experience have shown that just the opposite is often true. When asked why they change or end relationships with suppliers, a group of clients gave the following responses:

- 1% die or quit
- 3% transfer
- 5% give business to a friend
- 9% receive better prices
- 14% become dissatisfied with the product or service
- 68% believe that their supplier is indifferent and shows a lack of concern

The lesson to be learned here is to stay in touch with our customers and always be looking for additional ways to be of service. In other words, *treat our clients like prospects.*

Referrals

Referral prospecting is the best, most obvious and least understood of all the prospecting techniques. Salespeople who are unskilled at this technique are losing out on hundreds of potential satisfied customers and tens of thousands of dollars in sales and commissions.

In my experience, people are always willing to lend a hand to help out another person, whether a perfect stranger, friend, business associate or family member. So letting our customers, friends, business associates and family members know how much we value them by asking for referrals is a great idea and only one of the compelling reasons to develop our skills in this area.

Referred leads are easier to turn into customers. When we are able to use someone else's name in the first few moments of a telephone or personal call, the prospect is much more likely to listen to us and not reject our approach out of hand. In addition, referred leads become customers up to five times as often as nonreferred leads. Because there is some type of credibility established, the referred lead is often presold on us. Referred leads also tend to become more loyal clients and are more likely to refer us to more prospects. Finally, utilizing referral prospecting saves time as less time is spent on prospecting.

To give a personal example, at one point one of my key clients decided to become less active. One-third of my income in the previous year was based on business from this client, and the notice of the change was quite sudden (thirty days). I knew that either I would have to lower my expectations or find some new clients in a hurry. Now, I am not afraid to pick up the phone and call cold, yet I needed to jump-start my prospecting efforts. So I called three of my best clients, explained the situation and asked for referrals in three selected industries and if I could mention them as satisfied clients. The net result was three new clients in less than sixty days.

Ask for the referral in a specific manner. It has been said that once we reach adulthood we can recall almost 2,000 people on a first-name basis. Asking, "Do you know anyone I might call?" is therefore too vague and likely to result in a failed attempt. The right way to prospect on a referral basis is to be specific about the type of company and contact we're interested in. We're attempting to focus the person's attention on a particular person or industry. For example:

> "John, I've decided to offer my products and services to locally owned, neighborhood banks in our city. Who do

you know over at Town Bank, Corner Savings or one of the other banks in town? It could be the president, a loan officer, or an officer of the bank."

We should ask for a referral whenever we feel it is appropriate. For example, at the end of a phone contact with a client or prospect, after a successful sales presentation, after a sale is completed or after an order is shipped and received favorably. Other circumstances could be after a lost sale, or after a client or prospect tells us how much our product or service has been of benefit to them. Here is a model to follow when asking for a referral.

A MODEL REFERRAL REQUEST TO A CURRENT CLIENT

Step 1. Transition

"Before we get off the phone (or finish our meeting) today, there's one more matter I'd like to discuss with you."

Step 2. Compliment

"We've been working together for ____ now and I really enjoy our relationship. You're one of my most valued clients, and I want to thank you again for all the business you've given me."

Step 3. Reason

"As you may know, it takes a lot of time to give the type of service that you've come to expect from me, and while I'm perfectly capable of picking up the phone and calling on hundred strangers, I've found that my best new customers are typically referred to me by my current clients."

Step 4. Request

"So I'd like to ask you to do me a favor and help me. Specifically I am looking for a referral from you to people (or companies) such as (or like) ____________. Who do you know at (specific company or industry) ________________?"
(Never suggest one of their competitors!)

If They Give the Referral

"Thank you very much. I take your confidence in me very seriously and I'll treat (referral) ___________ with the same care and courtesy that I give you. I'll call you and let you know how everything went. Thanks again."

Send a personal thank you note immediately.

If They Don't Have a Referral to Offer

"Thanks for thinking about it. Give me a call if you think of someone, and I'll make a note to ask you again the next time we talk. Thanks again for your business."

WARREN WECHSLER'S 85-11-68 RULE

I created the "85-11-68 rule" to further illustrate how important referrals are. In a study done in the late 1980s, 85% of the surveyed clients were satisfied with their current supplier and willing to give referrals to their salesperson. The study went on to show a second, alarming statistic — only 11% of the salespeople in the survey ever asked the client for a referral. Add to the 85% and the 11% statistics the fact that 68% of people change suppliers because they think that their supplier is indifferent and shows a lack of concern, and you have the 85-11-68 rule. Keep the clients happy, keep in touch, ask for referrals and treat your clients like fine treasures.

One great way to do this is by conducting a Current Client Contact Program.

Current Client Contact Program: It's as easy as 1, 2, 3

This is a program that I developed for a division of one of the largest banks in the United States and have used successfully in my own business and with dozens of my clients. Some of my clients increased their sales by 30% and more once they mastered and applied this approach. It's simple and it works. It makes a great campaign.

A Current Client Contact Program accomplishes three things. First, it helps us find business that we can get right now. Second, it helps us set up follow-up calls in a timely manner for future business. Third, it's a perfect way to move into a referral request or discuss new opportunities with our clients. Here's how it works. Call one of your clients, and after you've warmed up the call or reintroduced yourself, ask them the following three questions:

1. "What can I be doing for you *now*?"

This question establishes an opportunity for new or additional business as well as keeps you in touch to let them know you care. After the now is taken care of and especially if no immediate needs were discovered, then go to question 2.

2. "It's important to me that my clients know I care about them. I call some of my clients once a week, some once a month, some quarterly and still others based on needs coming up on the horizon. *When* should I be in touch with you again?"

This is your opportunity to establish a call back date, future need keep in touch strategy. Then move on to the last question.

3. "There's *one more reason* that I called you today...." Either move into referral request, close for a face-to-face appointment or introduce a new product, idea or service that other clients are buying or showing interest in.

This question is your opportunity for a referral or additional business.

Company orphans

Company orphans are closely related to current customers as a source of prospects. All companies have some turnover in salespeople. There are many people in your company files who no longer have a designated salesperson and who can be your direct link to their company as well as a resource for additional information and service. Why not call these orphans up and "adopt" them?

When I was in the office equipment business I was new to the city and new to the territory. I had no "who do you know" lists and no clients. So I copied all of the service records of all the established clients in my territory who had purchased equipment from a salesperson no longer with my company and had no new "designated salesperson" assigned to them. I called them up and said, "You've been a good client of my company. I notice that the salesperson with whom you did business is no longer with our company (or in a different territory or has been moved into another department). I'm calling to 'adopt' you as my client and let you know that I am here to help you with anything you need, from new ideas to service issues. Can I come out and introduce myself sometime soon?"

This simple technique, on an ongoing basis, accounted for about 20% of my business each month.

Other departments within your company

Talking to people in your own company can often lead to ideas for new applications, problems to be solved or identification of older or overused products and services. Many times our current customers are happy to talk to a service technician or administrative person about upcoming needs without the fear of being sold something. Many of the salespeople I've worked with have invested their own money and time in their coworkers who have opportunities to meet clients or prospects. They treat them to lunch or breakfast, or offer a "bounty" for leads that turn into additional business.

One time when I was a sales manager I started a "take a technician to lunch" program to encourage our salespeople to see if this strategy worked with people other than me. It worked very well. We sold lots of new and additional equipment. And in addition to the predicted increase in sales, two other unexpected and positive things resulted. First, the technicians and salespeople got to know each other on a more personal basis, and the usual tension between sales (the people who make the promises) and the technicians (who have to deliver on the promises) was reduced. Second, the technicians were happier because more of the outdated and hard to service equipment was removed from the field and replaced by newer equipment less likely to need extra service. A win for the salespeople, the technicians and the company.

Lead share groups

I've organized and participated in lead share groups with great success. I think it's one of the most exciting ways to develop new prospects. One of the lead share groups I organized and ran from 1986 to 1988, when I was in the commercial real estate business, included people from the office maintenance, construction/contracting, office furniture, telephone sales and installation, and computer industries. We all were interested in companies that were moving, expanding, contracting and so on. Our group generated over $400,000 in business over a two-year period for the six active participants. I know this because I tracked the statistics of who attended, how many leads were exchanged and what happened to the information.

I ran the group as a benevolent dictator (I think the people probably called me "Sarge" or "commandant" out of earshot). It took me about six months to weed out the people who were looking for a free ride and those who were not able or willing to assertively prospect for all of the participants. About ten to twelve people came and went until the core group of six was established. I'm no longer active with the group, but the last time I checked (in the spring of 1994), it included about fifteen people and tons of leads continued to be passed among the members.

Wouldn't it be great to have twelve eyes and ears and be able to be in more than one place at a time? With a lead share group of six active salespeople, you can do just that. Here's how. Find five noncompeting salespeople who are calling on prospects similar to yours, and then meet every other week to share information. As long as each person commits to bringing and not just taking information, it can be a very rewarding experience. Here are some rules to help your group be successful.

- Choose a consistent day, time and place to meet. Early mornings which do not interfere with prime selling times usually work best. For example, 7 a.m. to 8 a.m. is a good time. Weekly or twice monthly formats will work best. If you meet at a restaurant, each person should pay for their own meal.

- Begin and end on time.

- Keep the discussions positive, upbeat and informative and stick to business. If people want to discuss personal matters, they can come early or stay late.

- Five is the minimum number of participants and ten the maximum.

- Each person should commit to bringing two qualified leads to each meeting. People should plan on attending even if they don't have any new information to share. However, if certain individuals rarely bring leads, they should be asked to leave the group.

- When following up a lead, members should never use the referrer's name unless given permission to do so. Also, agree at each meeting who is going to work on which lead, and then communicate the results at the next meeting.

- If someone misses two meetings in a row without a valid reason and without advance notice, they should automatically lose their spot in the group unless all the other members agree to let the person stay for one reason or another.

Professional networking groups

Professionally run and managed networking groups are springing up all over the country. There is a fee to join, usually $300 to $500 for an annual membership plus breakfast or lunch dues. Some groups are better for a particular type of salesperson than others, so shop around until you find a group that represents the industries you would interact with best.

The groups meet weekly for 90 minutes, are scheduled either around breakfast or lunch, and have a formal format for sharing information. There is usually a fifteen minute informal networking period, followed by a ten to twenty minute presentation by a member on what he or she does, who they can help and what types of referrals they are looking for. Then the formal exchanging of leads takes place. Each member stands up, gives any leads and states in one minute who they are, what they do and what they're looking for. Most chapters use a three-part carbonless form to keep track of leads (one to the person who gives the referral, one to the person who receives the referral and one to the chapter for its records).

Most clubs have attendance requirements and minimum lead-sharing standards to keep people interested and active. Some networking groups also offer educational programs on selling, networking and the like, and conduct quarterly seminars, during which outside speakers are brought in and all the chapters from a major metropolitan area get together for massive networking opportunities that involve hundreds of people. For more information on opportunities in your area, check your library. (One example is Network Group, USA, 5200 Wilson Road, Suite 206, Edina, MN 55424, (612) 925-6005.)

Informal networking

There are many informal opportunities to network in social, business and civic settings. The goal is to share enough information with a potential client or referral source to enable you to determine if it would be a good idea to follow up later. There are six steps to follow to make sure that networking opportunities will work for you: prepare, greet, qualify, present, call for action and follow-up.

Prepare. Bring a positive, warm, enthusiastic and casual business manner with you. Nobody likes a shallow, sharklike approach to networking. Bring a supply of business cards and a pocket calendar so you can make a note of any future appointments you set up. A pen or pencil along with a small supply of

3 x 5 inch cards that can be written on discreetly are also helpful.

Greet. Introduce yourself and be proactive. Don't be afraid to approach small groups of people whom you've never met. If you attend social, business and civic events and attach yourself to people you already know, you'll miss out on numerous opportunities to network. If you approach a group of people who are engaged in conversation, simply stand close to the group where you can be seen, return any eye contact and wait for a lull or change of subject to introduce yourself or to be introduced. Ask people for their first and last names, and try to use them in your first few sentences so that you are comfortable calling them by name. Dale Carnegie said it in the 1930s and it's still valid today, "People's name are like music to their ears, and we ought to get in the habit of saying names in conversation as often as is appropriate."

A word of caution though. Using someone's name over and over again can be overdoing it. It's an art to use people's names appropriately without coming off as phony.

A warm, friendly and open approach will work best. It is customary in our culture (although not all cultures) to offer a handshake and maintain friendly, noninvasive eye contact. Initial discussions of lighter subjects such as the weather, noninflammatory current events or the reason you're at the event on that particular day are good conversation starters.

Eventually talk will come around to occupations. Be ready with a short, simple one to two sentence overview of what you do, who you represent and what makes it interesting. For example, I would say, "I am a sales and marketing consultant who specializes in helping salespeople and sales-driven companies increase their sales and enhance their professionalism. Mostly I become involved with sales training for individuals and small groups and do public speaking to organizations and associations. Tell me more about you."

The bridge statement back to the other person is important.

People like to talk about themselves. You'll develop a reputation as a good conversationalist and listener when you focus your conversations on the other person and what he or she does or is interested in.

Qualify. When it feels appropriate to find out more information or to probe for opportunities for yourself, ask innocent, open-ended questions that identify the person's current needs and situation, future needs and opportunities, and decision-making criteria. Keep it light, and if the interest seems to be there, move on to your presentation.

Present. You may decide to share, very briefly, a situation similar to what the person is describing to show how you were of service and offered some benefit. Then quickly move on to the next step.

Call for action. This is the point when you can ask for a card or some information about an appropriate follow-up. Offer one of your cards. If they don't have one, do not let them say that they'll call you. We want to maintain the initiative. In that situation, take out one of your cards, offer your pen and ask the person to write down their information on the back of it. When there seems to be a real interest, offer to meet, obtain information for them or to call them to set an appointment with them. Then close the conversation graciously, say thank you and move on! It's not fair to monopolize one person's time during these events. You may want to look for additional networking opportunities as well.

Follow-up. Send handwritten thank you notes within twenty-four hours to everyone who was helpful or friendly or who offered to do something for you. Remember, timing is everything. You never know when a well-timed thank you will help you in the short or long run. Keep it simple. For example:

> "Thanks for the opportunity to meet and visit with you yesterday at the (name the event). I enjoyed (mention

something specific about them, their situation or their company). Please expect a call from me in the next week so we can get to know more about each other."

I had a learning/teaching experience that is a good example of informal networking. One of my clients was a stockbroker who didn't see the benefits of informal networking so I challenged him to watch me in action. I had him join me at a Rotary meeting that was a joint meeting of five Rotary groups, almost 500 Rotarians in all. In just under an hour I initiated ten conversations that resulted in four legitimate prospects — all done in a professional, nonthreatening manner in a group that has strict protocol for solicitation of members. Within seven months I had developed two client relationships and several referrals from that one hour of networking.

Trade associations

Joining the trade associations of the industries that you are calling on is an excellent way to become known, be seen as an expert and generate leads. Too many salespeople only join trade associations that have as members their competing salespeople and companies, i.e., a commercial Realtor joining the association of commercial Realtors. While this may be a great way to meet your peers, develop new career opportunities and commiserate with your friends in sales, it is not the best way to develop business.

A better approach is to affiliate with the groups with which you want to do business and develop relationships. The commercial Realtor could join the printers association, the manufacturers trade association or the property division of the legal profession, for example. Many trade associations have associate membership status for companies that do business with their members. Ask your customers about the groups they belong to and find out when you can attend a meeting.

Chambers of Commerce

I urge salespeople to join their local chamber of commerce. It is a great way to network with other salespeople, business owners and professionals. Many chambers hold programs that exist solely for helping their members find opportunities to do business with one another. Business card exchanges, before- and after-hours social and educational programs, and new member blitzes are all great ways to meet people and expand a salesperson's sphere of influence.

Civic, service and other organizations

The local Kiwanis, Rotary, Lions and Toastmasters clubs are good ways to meet people, develop relationships and network for future business. A word of caution: Many of these organizations have strict rules about solicitation of members. Unlike trade associations, civic and service organizations exist to serve a need in the community or have other than business reasons for existence. You should have a true desire to be of service to whatever causes the club you join is involved in. Consider the business you gain as a byproduct, not a direct result of your membership.

I have found that joining one or two clubs at the most works best. It is also helpful to be a visible member by becoming involved in a leadership position, either as an officer or as part of the membership committee. I am an active member of Rotary International and Toastmasters International. I am a member to *be of service to the other members and the community.* The business I've done, while substantial, has come because a member grew to know me, found out what I did and who I helped, and then *approached me.*

PROSPECTING WHEN YOU ARE NEW TO A COMMUNITY

If you are new to a community or you have none of the campaign opportunities outlined above, don't panic! While it will be more difficult to get a quick start because there are not a whole lot of people who know and trust you, by applying the following ideas you will still get moving quickly enough. Try networking immediately, as soon as you start to know people. Use your networks as a campaign approach at the same time you use the following "cold call" approaches.

Daily newspaper

The best way for a salesperson to read a daily newspaper in any major metropolitan area is to put aside the front page (it's all bad news anyway, that's what sells newspapers) and move right to the business section. Most larger newspapers have a fairly good business news section, and some dedicate one day of the week for expanded coverage. Depending on your target market, you may find information that is useful once a week and at other times only once a month. Of special interest should be "people on the move" sections and "at the top" changes. I've used this source to develop quite a bit of business.

Here's what I did. I bought a pair of dressmaker scissors (they are also called pinking shears and they make a crinkle cut), a glue stick and some different colored construction paper. Whenever there was an interesting article regarding something of importance in an industry, a company or an individual I was calling on, prospecting to or doing business with, I would cut out the article with my fancy scissors, glue it to a colored piece of construction paper and mail it to the person along with my business card and a short note of congratulations, an FYI or whatever. When I followed up (within one week, never longer), I was amazed at the number of friendly responses, helpful advice and face-to-face appointments I got.

I know you're probably thinking that the people in the news are bombarded by phone solicitations, cards and letters, but you're wrong. Many of the people I sent articles to had not seen them. They were surprised that their associates, clients or other salespeople hadn't mentioned anything to them. In almost all cases, I was the only one who took the time to notice that they were in the news.

Even if you don't see anything of interest to cut out and send, reading the business section to stay informed is still a good idea.

Regional publications and journals

Many cities have weekly and monthly publications that are dedicated to following the business scene. Some of my best clients are doing business with me today because of an interesting article I read regarding them in one of these publications. As with the daily newspaper, I cut out an article or announcement, send it to the person with a few photocopies for their friends and associates, and enclose my card along with a short congratulatory note. Within a week I make a follow-up call to introduce myself. It always amazes me that I am usually one of the few people, and often the only one, to acknowledge the person's appearance in the publication.

Also, the *Wall Street Journal* is a good resource for the latest earnings reports of companies in your territory, which is a good conversation starter, particularly if the company is having a good year.

Local newspapers

For the same reasons mentioned above, I read the local community newspapers looking for useful information about people or companies that I have identified as good prospects.

Specialty publications

It seems like every manufacturer, distributor, retail, professional or service occupation has a newspaper, magazine or journal dedicated to it. From metalworking to accountants, from jewelry stores to banks, there is a publication filled with interesting articles about people and companies. Your customers and prospects can tell you what publications they read. The public library also has resource directories you can use to locate these specialty publications.

Yellow Pages

The Yellow Pages is wonderful for brainstorming lists of people and companies you might want to call on. When I decided to develop a prospecting campaign targeting the investment and brokerage firms in my metropolitan area, I simply wrote down the thirty-eight companies listed in the Yellow Pages, each on a separate sheet of paper. I wrote out five questions that I needed answered to determine whether the company was a good fit for me. Then I made my initial calls — cold with no contact names, just firm name, address and phone number straight out of the Yellow Pages. I made eight appointments from those thirty-eight companies and did business with three of them in the following six months.

From the full-page ads to the one-line listings and from A to Z, you can let your prospecting fingers do the walking. Using your strategic approach to your prospecting and implementing your campaign mentality, you could have the same success that I have had. I have worked with salespeople one on one numerous times, in my office and theirs, and have heard them tell me they didn't have good lists to call from, didn't have the money to buy one or some other excuse. (Usually their problem was the Theory of Too.) I'd ask, "Do you have a Yellow Pages handy?"

We'd then do a few minutes of brainstorming and come up

with two or three areas of potential prospects. I'd start dialing away. Every time I have done this I've identified at least two valid prospects in one hour of calling cold — no prequalifying, no names, just firm name, address and phone number.

Your local directory is easy enough to find. The larger public libraries even have the Yellow Page directories from most metropolitan areas as well as that for your city's suburban areas available for your use.

Other directories

There are many directories available. Here are some of the best with a brief description.

Contacts Influential. I call this directory the salesperson's Bible. Available for most major metropolitan areas, *Contacts Influential* lists all businesses by Standard Industrial Classification (a four-digit code that pinpoints businesses by type), zip code, street address and alphabetical order. There is also a key contacts section. The key attributes shown are the names of the key people, the number of employees and how long the company has been in business, in addition to the usual information such as address and phone number. There is a planning section that shows density by type of business and zip code, which helps in planning calls and saving time.

Contacts Influential can be leased on an annual basis and is also available in the public libraries. This directory works great once you've determined what your prospecting campaign will look like, making implementation rather simple.

Standard and Poor's. This directory contains descriptions of various publicly-held corporations, including those listed on the New York Stock Exchange, the American Stock Exchange and the larger unlisted and listed regional exchanges. *Standard and Poor's* contains detailed financial information on each company — sales, earnings, annual report data, balance sheet information, corporate background, subsidiaries and officer and director names. It is available at the public library.

Moody's Industrial Manual. This directory includes information on larger corporations, including those listed on the New York Stock Exchange, the American Stock Exchange and the larger unlisted and listed regional exchanges. Information on history, capital structure, businesses, products, plants and subsidiaries; names of officers and directors; and financial and operating data such as balance sheets, long-term debt and capital stock are all included. It is available at the public library.

Dun and Bradstreet Million Dollar Directory. This directory contains financial and management information on more than 160,000 public and private companies. Lines of business, sales volume, employee size, standard industrial classification and key decision makers are listed. Dun and Bradstreet also publishes other more specialized directories which focus on a specific industry group, for example electronics, consulting, health care and pension funds, to name a few. Canadian, British and other international information is also available. The Dun and Bradstreet directories are available at the public library.

Thomas Register. This is a multiple-volume directory that lists all the manufacturers in the country, alphabetically by category. Basic information such as company name, address and phone number as well as some information on product lines is included. If you are looking for companies that do any type of manufacturing, this is the place to look. It is available at the public library.

Reverse directories. Reverse directories allow you to work backwards from telephone numbers to find addresses and other information pertaining to each phone number in a given area. These are especially helpful to residential or personal service providers, such as Realtors, insurance people, direct sales or in-home sales type salespeople.

Construction newsletters

Construction newsletters are regional publications that are useful for learning a number of things. First, you can find out who is expanding or building. Additionally, you can get a feel for which areas are seeing the largest growth and target your prospecting efforts in selected geographic areas. The *Dodge Report* is an example of a construction newsletter. Many of these newsletters are purchased by and available at construction companies, lumber yards, general contractors and electrical, mechanical and plumbing contractors. Your library will be able to provide you with a list of construction newsletters in your area.

Reference libraries

Most communities have a reference library that focuses on business applications. It is usually located within the largest library in the area. Most libraries also have a business and economic section that has volumes of potential prospecting lists. Your best prospecting friend in the entire world is a knowledgeable librarian. Once you've developed your strategic prospect approach, determined your prospecting campaigns and identified the type of people and companies to approach, just go to a well-run major public library and share your story with the librarian. You'll walk away with a year's worth of prospects at no charge to you.

Universities and colleges

The local college or university system is another good resource for information and prospecting lists. Many have computerized databases that you can access, sometimes for a fee. Large amounts of information can be easily sifted through to glean a targeted list of prospects.

List brokers

These companies create, maintain and sell vast varieties of prospecting lists to businesses and individuals. Many of these firms have thousands of lists that, for a fee, can be customized for your particular application. The library is a good place to start to find regional or national directories of list brokers. Also look in the Yellow Pages for list brokers in your area.

Company newsletters

While you are waiting in a prospect or client's office, or when you are canvassing your area in person, be on the lookout for the company newsletters. They are usually filled with valuable information for the alert salesperson.

YOUR OWN NEWSLETTER

Because of the difficulty in maintaining regular and personal contact with large numbers of medium- or low-priority prospects, many salespeople publish monthly or quarterly newsletters to keep their names in the minds of their prospects. A newsletter should contain useful information, follow a standard format and always have a feedback mechanism such as a coupon, interest card or request for information card. This gives prospects perceived value. They also know what to expect and can easily communicate back to you. Always have your name, company, address and phone number prominently displayed.

SEMINARS

Conducting seminars is another effective way to build your prospect base. You can offer seminars to trade groups, buyers organizations or local chapters of associations that can use your products. If you can position yourself as an expert in an area that people are willing to explore in a public or semipublic forum, you can give people useful knowledge as well as an opportunity to become acquainted with you and the services you provide. Seminars are a long-term business builder.

YOUR EYES AND EARS

Using common sense and your eyes and ears can uncover a wealth of prospects. When driving around your neighborhood or territory, take a different route occasionally. You might notice an unusual level of activity, car lots filled to capacity, new homes going up and other movement. Do you think these would be areas to explore?

When you are between appointments and have some extra time, make a few canvass calls. Or easier still, when you have an appointment, make one call to the left and one call to the right of your appointment. These calls take less than five minutes and sometimes can pay you back in surprising ways.

When you read the paper, listen to the radio or watch television, do you pay attention to who is moving in or out of town, expanding their business or introducing a new product? Who is being promoted? Who is being honored or recognized? Who is getting married, having children, opening a new business, taking in a partner, retiring or has passed away? What trade shows are in town at the local convention center? Depending on your target prospects, some or all of these changes may lead to a good source of prospects.

Once you make the conscious decision to look around your world with prospecting in mind, you'll be amazed at how many opportunities you'll find for potential new clients. And remember, we always strive for *too many prospects.*

IN-PERSON PROSPECTING

Closely related to using your eyes and ears is the in-person prospecting technique. Stopping in at the local bank, hardware store, barber shop, beauty salon, gas station, convenience store and supermarket to ask questions about businesses and individuals who fit your prospecting campaign criteria is a great way to learn about potential prospects. Be as specific as possible and ask "who do you know who..." instead of "do you know anyone...."

For example, when you stop into the local bank, ask for the bank president and then say:

> "My name is ________________. I am a salesperson with National Cleaning Supplies. Our company helps companies do environmentally-safe maintenance of their manufacturing plants and saves them money at the same time. I've brought a list with me of the local manufacturers in town. Can you introduce me to the owners or plant managers at one of these companies or any others you're aware of? Thanks."

Here's another example. One of the most successful municipal bond salespeople I know used this technique with an interesting twist. He would drop in on the local barber shop, hardware store, gas station and other smalltown businesses in North Dakota, South Dakota and Montana, and say, "My company has a bond offering available that is paying a competitive yield and requires an investment of $500,000. Are you interested?" After the laughter would subside, he would ask, "Seriously, who in town has that kind of money?"

It worked every time and helped this salesperson identify the wealthiest individuals by simply walking up and down the street.

PRIORITIZING YOUR PROSPECTS

Once you develop your list of prospects, it is important to rate them by relative potential and importance. This is more an art than a science, and after you begin to contact some of your prospects you may change your initial rating.

The easiest and best way to prioritize the list is to apply the simple method of A, B, C. "A" prospects are the best in terms of volume of business, timeliness and strategic importance. Spend 50% of your time prospecting to your A people, who should be the top 20% of your prospects.

Spend 30% of your time prospecting to your "B" prospects, who should be the next 30% of your prospects, and spend the remaining 20% of your time with the 50% of the prospects left over. This will result in personal contact of your A prospects up to once a month (sometimes more often), your B prospects four to six times a year and your C prospects one to three times a year.

CALLING ON THE BEST PROSPECT NEXT

Making the approach to the right types of people, companies and industries can set you up for greater success in selling. What we want to always be doing is calling on our best prospect next. There is never a good reason for saving good prospects for later. I've heard people make statements like, one of these days I'm going to call on so and so. What happens is that "one of these days" is always in the future and when that salesperson finally gets around to calling on so and so, a different type of salesperson who also recognized the opportunity and made the call has already developed the relationship.

BUILDING YOUR PROSPECTING FILES

After you've made the commitment to have too many prospects and begin making your initial contacts, you'll soon find that you become overwhelmed by information. You will be at a loss as to how to organize the data and when to call back the prospect based on what you've found out. Many times early in my selling career I missed out on an opportunity simply because the necessary information was lost in my jumble of disorganized paperwork or I failed to call back at the appropriate time. The solution is not the problem it first appears to be — as long as you follow some basic rules.

First, you must remember to keep the information regarding "when" and "what" in two distinct systems.

The "when" information is the chronological course of follow up that you'll determine once you speak with the prospect and decide what the correct course of action will be. A daily planner is your "when" file, the "holding area" for the appropriate day, week or month for your follow-up. The only information needed is the name of the prospect.

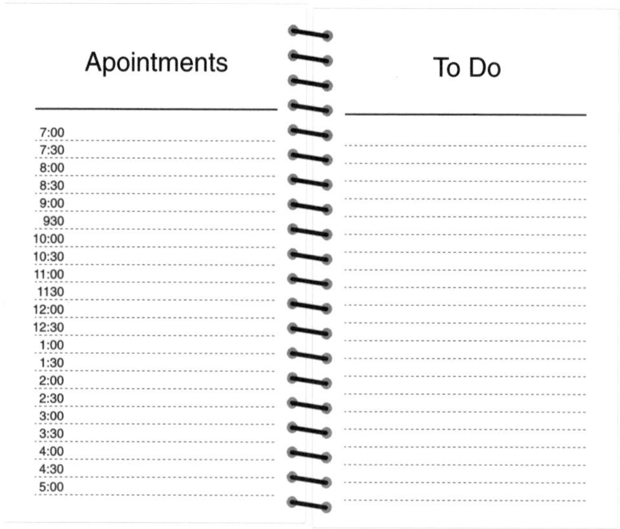

Apointments	To Do
7:00	
7:30	
8:00	
8:30	
9:00	
930	
10:00	
10:30	
11:00	
1130	
12:00	
12:30	
1:00	
1:30	
2:00	
2:30	
3:00	
3:30	
4:00	
4:30	
5:00	

For example, if ABC Company suggested during a phone conversation on April 24 that you should call on July 9 to schedule an initial face-to-face appointment, you would open your planner to July 9 and write in ABC. No other information is necessary.

Your "what" file is all the detailed information that you need to know about each prospect and client. You can create this prospect and client information system on 3 x 5 or 4 x 6 inch cards, on 8 1/2 x 11 inch sheets of paper or in a computer database. Make a list of the appropriate information you need to know about a particular prospect or client and then create your own format. Company name, phone, address, city, state, zip code, fax number, contacts and titles, assistants, secretaries, receptionists, type of business, SIC code, source code (where you found the prospect), applications, needs and so on can all be formatted along with lots of space for comments and follow-up steps.

Company ____________________ Phone ______________
Address ____
City __________________ State ______ Zip ____________
Decision Maker __________________ Title ______________
Other Contact __________________ Title ______________
Sec'y. __________________ Admin. Assist. ______________
Business Type ______________ Lead Source ____________
No. of Salespeople _____________ Sales Mtg. ____________
Outside Consultants? _____________________________

Date	Contacted	Type of Call	Follow-up/Action

It is critically important to keep these two information systems totally separate. If you keep the "when" information in your "what" files, you'll have to sift through your entire prospect information system every day or week to figure out who you should call. This is not a problem if you have a small number of people to follow up with, but once you start accumulating hundreds of prospects, you'll invariably lose track of people and miss many opportunities to develop business.

Some salespeople create their "what" files and then place them in a chronological follow-up system. This consists of tabs or file folders organized by months and within the months by days (1-31). If during an initial call on April 24, the prospects says to call back on July 9, the file goes in a "place holder" called July. The problem comes when the prospect calls back early. Because the entire record of information on this prospect is filed under July, the salesperson is in a very uncomfortable position, scrambling to figure out who the person is and what their history consists of (very unprofessional).

Another problem arises when the salesperson decides that there is a valid or new reason to call the prospect back before the agreed on date. The salesperson is reduced to rifling through record after record to find the prospect information (a waste of valuable time).

The only way to avoid these problems is to keep the "when" and "what" files completely separate. In this way, you will be able to track who you're calling when, and you'll have at your fingertips, and easily accessible, all the information you'll need to make the most of every contact you make.

Whichever format you use, each prospect file should be filed alphabetically. So if you decide to use cards, you'll need a card file with twenty-six tabs labeled A to Z. If you use sheets of paper, you'll need either a loose-leaf notebook with twenty-six tabs or file folders labeled A to Z.

Some salespeople further divide their prospect files by geographic location. This makes it easy to take additional files along when they have appointments in the area, so they can fill time between appointments or make a quick phone call for an appointment.

Once the amount of information on a particular prospect grows, you will probably decide to start a another file on the prospect and place it alphabetically in your client/live prospect/ in-process filing system.

WORKING WITH YOUR LISTS

Many of your prospecting lists will be photocopies or pages from directories. Once you start calling, you'll need to develop a system of managing the information involving who you called, how good the list is, who you transferred to a prospecting card/file and so on. One way is to categorize the people or companies on the list as:

- Valid prospects (warm leads)
- Not interested (cold or dead file)
- Not contacted (unknown value)

What I've done in the past is to simply use a ruler or straight edge to guide my eye when I'm making calls and keep a highlighter, dark marker, pen and prospecting card handy. As I make a call, I classify the contact by (1) using my pen to fill out a prospecting card and the highlighter to the mark the name on the list, (2) crossing out the name with my dark marker when I recognize that there is no interest or no potential, or (3) leaving the listing unmarked because the person is not available or I didn't learn enough to make a determination.

I use this approach for two reasons. First, I have a controlled method to move good information into a follow-up and prospecting system immediately; and second, at a glance I can tell how good my list is by the relationship of highlighted to black marks to blanks.

Now you have a plan for generating your own list of prospects. You know where to find them, how to find and organize them, what to do and why it is important.

ACTION PLAN FOR STEP ONE

Action 1: Create a prospecting campaign of three to eight concurrent strategies.

Prospecting Campaigns Planner

My prospecting campaigns are:

1. ______________________________

____

2. ______________________________

____

3. ______________________________

____

4. ______________________________

____

5. ______________________________

____

6. ______________________________

____

7. ______________________________

____

8. ______________________________

____

____

Action 2. Create a prospecting planner for each campaign.

Prospecting Planner

My target prospects (companies) groups for campaign number _________ are:

To develop a list of target prospects, I will use the following resources:

Action 3. Develop an A-Z and self-management system (what and when files).

"Prospecting Time" Planner

Scheduled activities drive out unscheduled activities.

Prospecting Schedule for the Week of ________________.

	Monday	Tuesday	Wednesday	Thursday	Friday	Saturday
7 a.m.						
8 a.m.						
9 a.m.						
10 a.m.						
11 a.m.						
Noon						
1 p.m.						
2 p.m.						
3 p.m.						
4 p.m.						
5 p.m.						
Evening						

2 The Second Step — Find the Decision Maker

As we learned in the previous chapter, the first step in building a successful selling career is to build our prospect base by finding the best prospects to approach. Once that is completed and we have a good list of potential clients, it is time to begin contacting those people and companies and obtain some additional information. Step Two is when we begin our detective work, looking for clues that will help us decide if we made good choices in our prospecting efforts. We need to learn how the target prospects make decisions, who is involved in decision making and whether it is appropriate for us to call on them. In essence, we begin to qualify the prospects we've identified to determine if they have the potential to grow into client relationships. Because we're operating under the assumption of having too many prospects, we can afford to have many of these initial contacts drop by the wayside. In fact, we expect this to happen.

Finding the decision maker and establishing buying (or qualifying) criteria is very important. This will save us time, money, potential aggravation and disillusionment later in the sales process. Why? Taking the time to do some of this qualifying, or detective work, on the front end of our approach to potential clients reduces time wasted on calling the wrong person and making inefficient calls.

For example, how often have you spent a substantial amount of time with a "good" prospect only to learn that you are talking to the wrong person? Down the road you learn that the manager of the training department makes all buying decisions, and you've spent your time doing a needs analysis, presentation and proposal for the marketing department. Or maybe you've called on that branch office of a large company and then found out (too late) that the decision is made at headquarters, which is out of your territory.

The point is that we need to dig for prospect information before we make the initial approach. So the detecting we do in Step Two is vital. We need to find out who makes the decision, and whom we should invest our time in.

THE THREE ATTRIBUTES OF A QUALIFIED DECISION MAKER

The three areas of information concerning our potential prospects that we need to dig for are need, authority and money.

Does the company need our products and services?

The first thing we should look at is the prospect's need for our products. Do they use our types of products and services in sufficient quantity to make a relationship between us worthwhile for them and us both?

Let's say you were a vegetarian, and I called you on the phone to discuss my premium line of steaks. I could describe in great detail the wonderful flavor, how the steaks were aged, the free shipping and on and on. At some point you would probably scream into the phone, "I'm a vegetarian, you idiot!" and hang up. Such an abrupt ending could befall our sales approach if we failed to ask a few preliminary questions and make some introductory comments to our prospect.

It is important to remember that this issue of need is a

two-way street. As we learned in Step One, our client make up and what we want to build in our sales career are based on our own unique prospecting campaigns. We have an idea, therefore, of what we are looking for. Sometimes we will face a situation in which the immediate need of the potential client is not sufficient to warrant our efforts. Situations such as low volume, low potential for re-orders, low margins or high servicing demands pose some tough questions that demand answers.

- How busy are we? (Too busy to pursue this business?)
- What is the likelihood that this might turn into something that will help us reach our goals? (What's the long-term view?)
- What is the potential for referral business or for leveraging what we would learn by taking on a marginal client? (Future, uncertain benefits to us?)

We need to determine if we really need this prospect. Sometimes we'll eliminate prospects from our prospecting base because they're not qualified to do business with us.

Who has the authority to make the buying decision?

The second area we look into during Step Two is which person or combinations of persons have the authority to make a decision regarding our offerings. A prospect's decision-making process can sometimes be simple and at other times very complicated. The point to remember is that you're looking for the person with the authority to answer yes to the ultimate question in the sales process: "Can we do business?"

Organizations have different ways of handling responsibility for buying decisions. Once we understand the process of a particular prospect, we are able to proceed appropriately. The theme that I try to apply is *aim high and aim appropriately.* If you are selling maintenance supplies to a Fortune 1000 company, it is unlikely that the president is involved in the decision, so calling and asking for the president is inappropriate. In a small company though, you may want to contact the president. Experience will be your best teacher.

It's best to establish in your own mind who you think would make the decision and start your approach with that person's supervisor. Then you're either speaking with the right person or you can be referred to the right person or persons. It's a lot easier to call someone when you can say, "I was just speaking with Mr. Jones (your boss) and he asked me to call you," than it is to contact a decision influencer (more on this later) and have to move up in the organization — or worse, to have this person become your spokesperson in their organization instead of you.

In my experience, and based on the type of selling I enjoy, most of my time is spent calling on presidents and owners of companies. One time I called on an office equipment company and asked to speak with the president. I introduced myself and applied the appointment setting program, which I'll explain later. The president told me that what I was saying made a lot of sense and would I please follow up with the sales manager. I replied, "Mr. Johnson, I'd look forward to the opportunity to meet with Mr. Olsen, your sales manager, and explain how my ideas might be of value to your company. Before I do that let me ask you a question. If Mr. Olsen likes everything I have to say and decides that your company can benefit from doing business with me, can Mr. Olsen commit the company's funds and say yes?"

The president replied that the sales manager did not have that authority and would have to discuss it further with him. I followed by saying, "Mr. Johnson, that's exactly why I would suggest that the three of us get together and discuss my ideas. What do you say?" After a long pause, which seemed like an eternity, the president said okay and set the appointment with me. The company became a client at that initial meeting.

Why did this happen, why did it work and why should the

professional salesperson learn this skill?

There are two major reasons. First, people are busier these days than ever before. Increased competition, downsizing of companies and multiple demands on all of us (family, career, exercise, social, spiritual, civic, etc.) make time the most valuable asset that any of us has. Why waste this precious commodity by being a weak salesperson and meeting with people who can only say no or maybe?

Secondly, who is the best person to be the advocate for your company, your products, your services, your solutions and your success stories? Who is best at finding out what the potential client needs? You or the person who has to gather information and discuss it with the true decision maker? And who knows best what the mission of a company is and how best to accomplish it? It's the decision maker and that's who we want to be in front of.

When I was a sales manager, I tracked the success rate of salespeople's calls, comparing those whose initial calls were to the decision maker with those whose calls were made on people who could only say no or maybe, people I call "decision influencers" (more about them later). I found that if the call was to a decision influencer and the decision influencer asked three potential vendors or suppliers to come in and make presentations, we had a slightly better chance than one out of three to obtain the commitment to do business. If there were six potential vendors or suppliers, we had a slightly better chance than one out of six to get the commitment to do business. The point is that when we were not calling on the decision maker, we were not being our best advocate, and it was just like rolling the dice — mostly luck.

Conversely, when the salesperson called initially on the decision maker and declined to meet with people other than the decision maker, our success rate as one of three to six vendors was consistently around 50%.

Too many times I've watched salespeople lose their conviction and confidence while allowing other people to control their destiny. Although I may be staking out an extreme point of view here, I made a decision early on in my sales career to call on decision makers, and my successes have far outweighed my failures using this approach.

Who controls the money?

The third attribute of a qualified decision maker is that he or she controls and will spend the appropriate amount of money. We can have the best products, services and customer support in the industry, but if the prospect cannot or will not work out the financial obligations, or does not have the necessary budget to buy our products, then we are wasting our time. In smaller companies run by entrepreneurs who like to make decisions, we may not have to probe any further to find the money. In other organizations, we may have to develop additional contacts to learn what combination of people and circumstances need to come together for us to obtain a yes when we eventually ask for the business.

As with a three-legged stool, we're likely to fall off our seats if we try to move forward in the sales process without the balanced base of a qualified prospect with the attributes of need, authority and money.

TITLES OF DECISION MAKERS

Smaller companies usually have a person with the title of owner, president or partner who makes most decisions that will affect the company's image or balance sheet. When calling on smaller companies, always ask for this person by title.

Most larger companies organize responsibilities by departments. Knowing which departments to call on is a helpful start in finding out who has the authority within an organization. Some likely places to start are the executive offices, human resources, marketing or purchasing departments.

For smaller ticket items and for purchase requirements up to a certain dollar level, some companies delegate the authority to buy to decision influencers. In these cases, the qualifying approaches explained later in this chapter will help us determine the right level of contact in an organization.

As a rule of thumb, aim as high and appropriately as possible. Look for the following titles.

In smaller companies:

- President
- Owner
- Principal
- Partner
- Vice president
- Officer

In larger companies (in addition to those listed above):

- Departmental manager
- Managing partner
- Other corporate officers (secretary, treasurer)
- Controller
- Director

DECISION INFLUENCERS

I've defined decision influencers as people who often are involved in the decision-making process but who only have advisory or influencing roles. Most of the time these people can say no or maybe, but in almost all cases they need to speak with someone else before saying yes. It is important to treat these people with respect and acknowledge their role in the process, but at the same time let them know that you want to be included in the decision-making loop as well. This skill is more an art than a science. One way to establish if a person is a decision influencer or decision maker is to ask questions like, "In addition to you, who is involved in decision making?" This gives the person credit for being part of the process. In most organizations, the following people will likely be decision influencers:

- Assistants
- Office managers
- Supervisors
- Executive secretaries
- Administrative assistants
- Secretaries
- Untitled persons

Working with decision influencers

Most top salespeople know that secretaries (as well as receptionists, administrative assistants and the like) are the salesperson's ally. Unfortunately, many salespeople fail to recognize this important fact. Instead, they think of all kinds of ways to get around this person, assuming that the only role this person plays is that of "salesperson screener" or "gatekeeper." Establishing a good relationship with secretaries, including remembering and using their names, will often help a salesperson get through to the right people in the long run.

Just recently I decided to call on a large regional securities company. I had read an article in the local paper about some of their recent issues and problems. The CEO was quoted in the article, and even though I thought I'd probably be referred to someone else, I decided to aim high and appropriately. I called his secretary to give me some insight into the company. I introduced myself and said that she probably received a lot of calls so I would be brief and to the point. Based on my respectful approach, she trusted me. In five minutes this woman told me exactly who I should know, who reported to whom and how the hierarchy in the company worked as it related to training and consulting needs.

Of the four names she gave me, I was unsure where to start so I asked her what she would do if she were me. After a long pause, she said to call on the senior vice president. Although he was not the true decision maker (he was too high up), he would refer me to number two. This is exactly what happened. The appointment was scheduled for the next week, and I made the sale on the spot!

By the way, I thanked her during our conversation and sent a thank you note immediately after our phone call. I followed up with another phone call as soon as I made the connections to let her know how helpful she was. She thanked *me* for calling on her company!

Once you establish who you're going to call and at what level in the organization you're going to make your initial approach, become acquainted with the secretaries, assistants and receptionists. Introduce yourself, take names, send thank you notes and ask them to help you reach the appropriate person. Treat them with respect and you'll reap huge dividends.

MIND YOUR QQTS — QUALITY, QUANTITY AND TIMING

There is another way of looking at identifying the people and companies who are going to be privileged to be in your prospecting universe. It's what I call "Minding Your QQTs — Quality, Quantity and Timing." This is more a philosophical or strategic way of qualifying prospects than a tactical approach of who has the need, authority and money.

Notice the use of the word "privileged" in the above sentence. Many people carry negative attitudes around with them about salespeople. We all saw the Isuzu truck TV commercials in the late 1980s where "Joe Isuzu," a slick fast-talking salesperson, would make outrageous (obviously false) claims about the Isuzu truck. The television viewer was instructed to see the Isuzu dealer for the true details.

And who can forget "Herb," the radio sales rep on the sit com "WKRP in Cincinnati," who wore the loud, plaid sports coat and was constantly acting irresponsibly, bordering on unethical?

We even have to endure comparisons to Richard Nixon in his infamous days (Would you buy a used car from this man?) and hear the jokes like:

> Question: "How do you know when a salesperson is lying?"
> Answer: "His/her lips move." (Ha, ha)

If we let ourselves, we could get pretty depressed about our chosen profession. Yet the reality of the life of the professional salesperson is just the opposite. He or she is an invaluable part of any economy. Goods and services would not be bought or sold unless a salesperson first made the call and discovered the need. As Red Motley said, "Nothing happens until someone sells something!" So our attitude must be that any person, company or industry group that we determine to be in our prospecting universe is privileged to have the potential opportunity to develop a business relationship with us. Imagine how effective we will be and confident we will sound when we approach people with that frame of mind!

The **quality** in QQT means that the person or company we approach has the principles, ethics and business values that we believe are important. Being treated fairly and honestly, having phone calls returned promptly, not being verbally or sexually harassed, and being told all the relevant facts are examples of what I mean. There are so many companies and people who would benefit from our products and services that we only hurt ourselves and our self-image if we let people beat up on us. There is plenty of legitimate rejection in a selling career.

To have inappropriate negatives dumped on us too is not good for us, our prospects or our customers. We have a right as a professional salespeople to walk — or run — from this type of person or business.

One of my clients had a particularly mean, dispirited and abusive customer who represented about 25% of this salesperson's revenue. The client sapped all of this salesperson's drive, energy and enthusiasm. My advice, which he followed, was to aggressively prospect to more and more people while still doing business with the curmudgeon (no need to starve and not meet quota while his script was being rewritten). When he developed enough new business to make this mean person's business rather insignificant, I told him he should resign the account. This is just what happened. This salesperson became the number one salesperson in his company and has never been happier in his career.

The **quantity** in QQT means that the prospect has enough potential to warrant us calling on him or her. In every business there is a maximum or perfect number of clients that can be maintained before the level of service breaks down or the salesperson feels that the promised quality begins to erode. Therefore, each salesperson needs to evaluate how many new clients he or she can accommodate and how much quantity or volume each prospect needs to be able to bring to the table to make the relationship valuable and profitable for the salesperson and the potential client.

A word of caution — make sure when you do this analysis that you look at the entire potential. A small initial relationship with the potential to grow significantly in the future is a pretty good prospect that could be overlooked if you're just considering today's dollars. It's important to balance the short-term need to make this month's quota or goal with the longer term issue of what your business should look like in the future.

The **timing** in QQT means that if the prospect passes the tests for quality and quantity, then it will just be a matter of timing for us to do business. This gives the salesperson an opportunity and a reason to practice persistence. If I know that a prospect is the right kind of person or company and has the potential volume, either now or in the future, that is good for me, then I'll call until the prospect says either yes or get lost forever! Studies have shown that the best accounts are typically opened after a combination of five to seven contacts and approaches. The scary part (or exciting part if you are one of the persistent ones) is that most salespeople make two calls and then give up. Just look at the potential for us if we mind our QQTs!

THE QUALIFYING APPROACH TO FINDING THE DECISION MAKER

Our goal is to ask enough questions during a quick initial phone call (or in-person call) to learn the answers to our own unique decision-making criteria. The best approach is a planned approach. In my experience there are usually no more than five questions that need to be asked on this initial call. Here are some examples from my current and previous businesses.

Consulting and Training

1. Who is the president or owner (or general manager if a branch or franchise)?
2. How many salespeople in this location? Nationally?
3. When are their sales meetings? Frequency, location?
4. Have they ever used outside consultants/speakers in the past? Examples?
5. Who else is involved in the management/motivation of the sales staff?

Commercial Real Estate

1. Who is the president or owner (or general manager if a branch or franchise)?

2. Tell me about your current real estate situation. Own, rent, square feet, terms, special needs?
3. Considering any changes in next two years? Expansion, downsizing, branches?
4. Worked with any brokers in the past? Who, why, currently involved?
5. When will any longer-term space needs be evaluated? And by whom?

Office Equipment

1. Who is the president or owner (or general manager if a branch or franchise)?
2. What type of copier/fax do you currently use? Rent or own? Term?
3. Considering any changes in next six months?
4. Usage: copies per month, paper, etc.?
5. Who else gets involved in evaluating the office equipment trends, needs, etc.?

You can see that as long as I know what I'm looking for, I can get a pretty good idea in just about five minutes if I want to pursue this prospect.

Example of an initial approach

Let's look at a possible initial call made by someone who sells binders, notebooks and training manuals. This call might be made to the receptionist, departmental secretary or administrative assistant. It also will work when calling on the true decision maker.

> "Good morning (afternoon). This is ___________ calling with ABC Company, a custom binder and notebook manufacturer."

"Who is the president or owner of your company?"

"Who else in your organization is responsible (involved in) the development of training materials (binders, procedure manuals, etc.)."

"What is their title, please? To whom do they report? Great. May I speak with them please? Thank you!"

Later, when you have the decision maker on the phone:

"Good morning (afternoon). This is _______________ calling with ABC Company, a custom binder and notebook manufacturer. I've been given your name as the person responsible for _____________. I'd like to ask you a few questions that will take five minutes of your time. Okay?"

Make sure that they have the time. Be sensitive to their schedules. If the person asks, "How much time will this really take?" then respond, "I will only require five minutes unless you have questions of me or if you have an immediate interest in additional information."

"What type of manuals, (binders, training materials, etc.) do you currently use? Quantities?"

If none, ask:

"When was the last time that you had a need for them?"

Followed by:

> "Do you anticipate that you will be using them in the future?"
>
> "From who do you purchase your binders? Who is your current vendor?"
>
> "Are you currently considering any projects?"
>
> "When you do have a use for binders, how many do you usually need and what lead times do you work with?"
>
> "One last question. Who else in your organization would be involved in these types of decisions? What is their title (relationship to you)?" "Thank you very much. Good bye."

If you have the decision maker on the phone and the conversation is going well, so you feel that there is a compelling reason to continue the conversation, it is appropriate to bridge to the next step — arranging an appointment. If this is the case, say:

> "You're just the type of company that can benefit from some of my company's ideas. When might we get together and discuss some ideas?"

If you're not speaking to the decision maker, ask to be connected to the appropriate person and review what you found out.

ACTION PLAN FOR STEP TWO

Action 1. Determine the types of decision makers you seek.

Decision-Maker Criteria Planner

The decision makers I am looking for will have the following attributes:

Size of Company	Title	Need	Authority	Money
Larger/Smaller		Yes/No	Yes/No	Yes/No

Action 2. Write your qualifying approach.

Qualifying Planner

APPROACH (When receptionist answers phone)

Good morning (afternoon). This is _______________ calling with (company name), a _______________________________.

Who in your organization is responsible for (involved in) the search for (use of) __________________________________.

What is their title please?
May I speak with them? Thank you.

QUALIFICATION QUESTIONS

Good morning (afternoon) Mr. (Mrs./Ms.) _______________.
This is ____________ calling with_______________ (company name), a _________________________. I've been referred to you as the person at ___________________(company name) who is responsible for (involved in) the search for (use of) ___________________. Is this correct?

Great. I'd like to ask you some quick questions that will take five minutes of your time. Okay? (Make sure that they have the time. Be sensitive to their schedules.)

(NOTE: If the person says, "How much time will this really take?" then respond: "I will only require five minutes unless you have questions of me or if you have an immediate interest in additional information.")

(action plan continued on next page)

1. ____

2. ____

3. ____

4. ____

5. One last question. Who else in your organization would be involved in these types of decisions? What are their titles (relationship to you)?

Thank you very much. Goodbye.

The Third Step — Arrange an Appointment

Building on our successes in the first two steps, we are ready to move on to Step Three, arrange an appointment. Before we can be actively involved in the selling phase of our business, we have to be face to face (or phone to phone) with qualified decision makers. In our enthusiasm to accomplish this, it's possible that we might try to push people into seeing us. We've all been approached this way one time or another. Remember how you felt when someone was overly aggressive or even borderline unethical in pursuit of an appointment with you? These manipulative, aggressive strategies are often unsuccessful, not to mention unprofessional.

In this chapter, we'll cover the positive, nonmanipulative, professional ways we can arrange appointments with people. There are some very effective opening statements we can use as well as creative approaches that will result in our goal of setting appointments.

My research has shown that many of the most profitable and loyal client relationships were started only after a face-to-face meeting between the salesperson and the prospect. But before this occurred, the salespeople had often spent too much time trying to sell their products and services over the phone, instead of trying to set up the appointment to meet face to face.

Buying a product or service is a personal and emotional decision for most people. Yet, many salespeople ignore this. Instead on the initial call they begin to press the issues of how their products and services will benefit the potential prospect. In other words, they begin to sell before it is appropriate. This is why Step Three is so valuable and important to master. Effective appointment-setting skills help the salesperson establish the initial credibility and rapport that leads to successful sales and satisfied clients.

One of my clients was new to selling when I observed her making phone calls. I noticed that she was telling her entire story on the phone and not trying to arrange an appointment. She shared knowledge of her company, products and services, trying to sell over the phone. Once she learned of the need to sell the appointment first, her success and progress were dramatic.

THE OBJECTIVES OF APPOINTMENT SETTING

Every time we pick up the phone or stop in to see someone, we must have a specific and measurable objective. That way, even if we are taken off course, we can keep our objective in mind and complete the call with a successful outcome. If we can't complete the sentence, "The reason I'm calling you today is..." then we have not learned the lesson of ECHO:

E - Every
C - Contact
H - Has (an)
O - Objective

These days people are busy and have multiple priorities. A planned approach with a clear agenda makes sense for us and the people we're calling. I'm not suggesting that we become cold and calculating, not warming up to people. I am suggesting that after the initial pleasantries have been exchanged (if the person we're approaching wants to warm up to business slowly), we have a plan for bridging to the business reason for our call.

Knowing how to position the appointment call in your mind as well as the mind of your prospect is very important. And it is a great opportunity to establish objectives. The objectives of the appointment setting call are to:

- Introduce ourselves appropriately
- Make an attention-getting statement
- Overcome reflex resistance
- Make a firm appointment

Introduce ourselves and our company

It is infuriating to many people to be asked questions by people who don't have the common courtesy and good sense to introduce themselves. Most of the time we fail to introduce ourselves (even to secretaries and receptionists) because we think that we are opening the door to immediate rejection. It is true that once we disclose who we are and who we represent, the prospect may begin immediately to say no. This is an example of "reflex resistance," a situation we will address below. But we still should introduce ourselves. For example:

> "Good morning, Mr. Smith. My name is Tom James, a salesperson with American Food Service."

Get attention with general benefit statement

Most people want the opportunity to save time, make time, save money, make money, enhance their image, increase sales, provide security, increase profits, reduce expenses, make things easier, have the latest technology and so forth. That's why after introducing ourselves, we move right into the reason we're calling. The strategy is to offer one or more benefits that people and companies will enjoy if they do business with us. An example:

> "The reason I'm calling is that I'd like to meet with you to share some ideas (mention some specific or general ones) that companies like yours (mention some) are using to save time (or save money, reduce costs, etc.) by working with my company."

Eliminate reflex resistance

We are usually interrupting people when we make the appointment-setting call. (It's not like they're sitting around saying, "Gee, I wish that nice salesperson from ABC Company would call me today.") It's not surprising that most of the time the initial response on the part of the prospect is, "Not interested," "I'm busy" or "No." You need to recognize the interruptive nature of this call and learn to be finely attuned to the initial responses, background noise, tone of voice and the like. Once we understand this, we can stop taking the initial reflex resistance personally, which is why most salespeople do not prospect enough. Over time, the experienced person develops a sixth sense and learns to be sensitive to busy people so he or she knows whether it's a convenient time to call and whether to ask for the appointment one more time or to wait until the next call.

Examples of countering reflex resistance are given later in this chapter.

Make a firm appointment

We're not selling anything on the phone except the appointment. While it may be our approach to lead with a point of view or a particular idea (competitive advantages, new technology, selection, service, delivery, personal attention, etc.), it is just a starting point to begin a dialogue with the prospect and to test for interest in one particular area. Having a face-to-face appointment or the opportunity to call again for that appointment is still our only goal. For example:

"When could we meet to discuss these ideas?"

USING LETTERS OF INTRODUCTION

Our success in arranging an appointment can often be enhanced through a letter of introduction. This alerts the prospect to the idea of receiving an appointment-setting call and gives the person a chance to recognize the salesperson's name, company name, logo, etc. Send a letter of introduction then follow it up by a phone call in two to three days.

Some salespeople find that a letter of introduction assists them in setting appointments. For others the letter makes less impact. To experiment, send letters to half of a target group and not to the other half. Then compare your appointment-setting results to find out if a letter of introduction is worth your time and expense.

Sample letter of introduction

This letter should be sent to the people whom the salesperson intends to call for an appointment. It is best to send out ten to twenty per day, wait two to three days and then follow up with a phone call. Included with this letter should be a business card and one small piece of information about the company. Envelopes should be hand-addressed with a real stamp, not run through a mail meter device. The result of this letter should be "warmer" appointment-setting calls.

A sample letter of introduction appears on the next page.

Date

Name
Company
Address
City State Zip

Dear Mr. (Ms.):

Thank you for this opportunity for me to introduce myself and my company. My name is ________________. I am with __________ (your company name), a ____________ (brief description of the business).

Our many satisfied customers (drop some names of satisfied clients, if appropriate) tell us that they have come to rely on ______________ (your company name) because of our ability to help them _____________________ (general benefit statement).

To see if there could be a mutually beneficial relationship between your company and _________ (your company), I would like to meet with you to discuss your current situation and needs. If, after a careful study of this information, it appears that I can be of service to you, I may outline a program of how we could work together.

You may find that spending a few minutes discussing these ideas with me might be to your benefit. Please expect a call from me in the next few days to find out when we might get together.

Sincerely yours,

Name
Title

PLANNED VS. CANNED OR "WING IT" APPROACH

As we discussed earlier, the ECHO principle states that every contact must have an objective. We need to be able to finish the sentence, "The reason I'm calling you today is..." with a convincing, logical and emotionally appealing statement. That's why I am such a strong advocate of a planned approach. It means that we know what we're going to say, what we're likely to encounter and what our ultimate objective is.

A "canned" approach, where the approach is scripted in writing and read word for word, is not usually effective for two reasons: first, because the prospect knows the salesperson is reading and not really personally interested in the prospect; and second, because if the prospect says something that is not in the script, the salesperson gets flustered and loses composure.

Neither is a "wing it" approach effective, again for two primary reasons. First, the objective is not clear and the salesperson runs the risk of missing out on key opportunities due to forgetfulness. Second, the prospect feels that the salesperson is wandering or just fishing with no sense of direction. The salesperson appears unprofessional and insensitive to the prospect's time.

THE OPENING AND THE THIRTY-SECOND RULE

The salesperson has thirty seconds to open the conversation and grab the attention of the prospect. My opening statement has been carefully fine-tuned over the years. It's simple, direct and fast. Warmly, enthusiastically and businesslike, I begin:

> "Good morning Mr. (Mrs./Ms.) ________________(I always use their last name). My name is Warren Wechsler. I'm the president of Total Selling Systems, a Minneapolis-based training and development firm dedicated to helping

> salespeople and sales-driven companies improve their sales performance with custom-designed individual and group programs. (When appropriate) I've been referred to you by ______________________. (Pause) Is this a convenient time for you to talk?"

SAMPLE APPOINTMENT-SETTING APPROACH

Here is a model you can follow for an appointment-setting call. As you will see, it is neither canned nor done "on the wing."

> "Good morning (good afternoon) Mr. (Mrs./Ms.) ____________. My name is ________________ with ___________ (your company name), a ___________ (brief description of the business)."

If you have been referred to this person, mention the referrer's name now. Then pause and listen for response. Silence will often let you know if you have caught the person at a bad time. You will eventually develop a feel for whether the person on the phone is willing to listen, in a hurry, not interested, etc.

> "Is this a convenient time for you to talk?"

> "The reason that I'm calling you today is because we've been able to help our clients (drop names if appropriate) ________ (pick one of three to four preselected general benefit statements that address how you help your clients save time, make time, save money, make money, enhance their image, increase sales, provide security, increase profits, reduce expenses, make things easier, have the latest technology, etc.)

This next sequence is the most important part of the approach. I was very frustrated during one particular day of appointment-setting calls. When one prospect began to offer some pretty serious resistance, I said, out of frustration, "Look, I don't know if I can help you or not. That's why I'm calling you for an appointment!!!!!"

After a long pause the person said, "Okay, come on in."

I've been using the technique ever since and only years later did I figure out why it works. People are used to salespeople calling them up and being pushy. "You really need this!" "Our company is really good!" "You should see this new gizmo!" The reflex resistance goes up in the mind of the prospect almost unconsciously. When we reduce the tension, the prospect naturally opens up, lets down their defenses and really begins to listen to us.

> "Now, I don't know if I can be of service to you or not, but I'd like the opportunity to meet with you to discuss ways that you can benefit from a business relationship with my firm."

Be quiet and listen for response!

> "When can we get together and talk about these ideas? (Agree on a time and day) That's great. Thanks in advance for the upcoming opportunity. To confirm, do you have a pencil handy? Pencil me in for next _______ (day) at ______(time). My name again is __________ (spell it) and my company and phone number are _________________ in case you need to reach me between now and then."

Some sales training specialists would scream at my suggestion to give the prospect your phone number. "They might cancel," they would say. If they don't have your number they can't cancel. I say hogwash to that. Remember, we want to be considered equal in stature to our prospect and professional. Imagine the perceived strength we carry when we are willing to let the prospect have a way to cancel or reschedule the appointment. They respect us and appreciate our valid concern that something might come up.

RESPONSES TO REFLEX RESISTANCE

All appointment-setting calls are not initially successful. (Not a big surprise here!) Reflex resistance is a natural response. Our goal is to not panic, but to listen and then respond appropriately. Demonstrate empathy (an understanding of how the prospect feels) by always beginning your response with one of the following statements:

- "I can appreciate that."
- "I understand how you feel."
- "I see your point."
- "I hear what you're saying."

Here are some sample responses to resistance from the prospect.

"No, not interested."

"Mr. (Mrs./Ms.)__________________. I can appreciate how you feel. You're probably wondering just who I am and why do I think that I could be of service to your company. All I'm asking for is the chance to show you why some of my best customers weren't interested the first time I contacted them and what they found out by spending just fifteen minutes with me. Would ____________ suit your schedule?"

"I understand what you're saying. Your downside risk when you meet with me would be spending just a few minutes in an unproductive manner. On the other hand, you may find that spending those few minutes with me might be of benefit to you, either now or in the future. Certainly that's worth some time to you isn't it? What would be a good day for you next week?

The following response will probe for the next call back date even if the prospect shows no interest.

"I understand that you are not interested right now. As a salesperson who provides a real service for my clients, I tend to walk a fine line between being persistent, which I want to be with you because I think I can be of benefit to you, and being a pest, which I do not want to be. When would it be appropriate to call you again?"

"How long will this really take?"

"That all depends on your interest. If it turns out that you have no interest and no questions, then I'll be out of your office in fifteen minutes. Only if you decide that my ideas can be of use to you will this initial meeting last any longer. When would you have fifteen minutes to get together?

"I already have a supplier."

"I can appreciate that. I am not calling to replace your supplier but only for the opportunity to share some ideas with you that might even result in better relations with your current supplier. Maybe you'll decide to do some business with me down the road, maybe not. All I'm asking is for some of your time to explore the possibility of something that may be beneficial to you. Would ____________ work for you?"

"Send me something in the mail."

If you don't want to do it, respond:

> "I can appreciate that. Because of the wide range of products that we represent, I feel that you'd only get part of the story. I take my client responsibilities and their confidence in me very seriously, and meeting you person to person is very important for me to get an understanding of your needs and priorities. What day next week would work best for you?"

If you must do it, respond:

> "I can appreciate that and I'll be happy to do it. After you receive it, and presuming you're interested, I'd ask for the chance to see you. I take my client responsibilities and their confidence in me very seriously, and meeting you person to person is very important for me to get an understanding of your needs and priorities. What day next week would work best for you after you've had a chance to look over the materials?"

"Call me next week."

> "It sounds to me like your pretty busy right now. I am too. I have my planner right here. Let's set something up for late next week, and I'll call to confirm our appointment. Would ____________________ be good for you?"

"We don't need... (your product). **We have** (other product or technology)."

> "It seems as though you have some good programs in place. New technology has made (our product) a lot more than just (other product or technology) and I can show you some of the new strategies used by companies like ______________________ in just fifteen minutes. When can we meet?"

MAINTAINING THE INITIATIVE (MTI)

The job of the salesperson is to be proactive and move the prospect throughout the six steps of the sales process. In general, maintaining the initiative means that as each phone-to-phone or face-to-face call is winding down, the professional salesperson is laying the groundwork and planting the seeds for the next call. Examples are setting the next appointment, establishing a call-back date and determining the date and time for a commitment. In this appointment-setting step specifically, there are many opportunities for the prospect to say, "I'll get back to you," or "We'll call you if we're interested." This also may happen at many different stages in the sales process. Our response is always the same and applies the principle of MTI — Maintaining the Initiative. We say,

> "That's great and I'll look forward to hearing from you then. If I don't hear from you by _______ (appropriate follow-up timeframe), then I'll make a note to call you back in ____________ (appropriate follow-up time-frame). Thanks again for your time."

Closely related to MTI is the issue of leaving our name and number so the prospect can get back to us. This is generally a bad idea. It puts the initiative in the prospect's arena. If they don't call (and many will not), we can seem overly aggressive if we call them back. Additionally, when the prospect does call back, the salesperson is likely to be on the phone or out of the office, anyway. Sales is a proactive business and my response to receptionists, secretaries and administrative assistants who ask me to leave my name and number is generally to say,

> "I'm in and out a lot (or on the phone a lot or out of the office a lot) so it's easier for me to get back with Mr. (Ms.) ______ . When is a good time for me to call back?"

SCREENS AS OBSTACLES

Sometimes we are faced with someone who either will not take our calls or has a person between them and people like us who are outside the company. In these cases, it is very helpful to appeal to the person's sense of fair play and ask for some understanding of our position. For example, we might say the following:

> "I have a problem. I need your help. I can appreciate that Mr. (Ms.) ________________ gets a lot of calls and you only want those that offer a true benefit to your company to get through. I think that I can be of genuine value, and in just ten minutes Mr. (Ms.) ________________ will know if my call is worthwhile. Maybe he/she comes in early, stays late or has as a short amount of time occasionally for calls like mine. When can I call and get three minutes of Mr. (Ms.) ________________'s time?"

HOW TO MAKE THE PROSPECT'S VOICE MAIL YOUR ALLY AND SELLING TOOL!

Voice mail can be an ally and an opportunity to develop relationships with people, but we need to learn how to work with it and recognize its benefits. Using voice mail to our advantage is both an art and a science. Like any part of the sales process, a planned approach will work best and get the best results. The rules are simple.

- Listen carefully to the voice mail message (standard, outdated or current).
- Make use of the live operator option (0, #0, *0, etc.).
- Ask the operator if the person we're calling is in or out and if the person has an assistant. If so, call that person to find out the schedule of the person you're trying to contact.
- If the person always uses voice mail, then talk to the voice mail as if it were a real person. In you initial approach, use ECHO principle and the four-step model below.

Step 1. Introduction

"Good morning (afternoon) Mr. (Ms.) ____________. This is ______________ calling with (your company name and a short description of your business.)"

If referral:
"I've been referred to you by __________________."

Step 2. Reason for the call

"The reason I'm calling is to find out if and when we could get together to find out if I can be of service to you. I don't know if I can help you and that's why I'm calling — to see when we might schedule a brief meeting to explore the possibilities."

Step 3. Statement of why the person might want to see us

"Many of our clients (mention some key clients if they will have name recognition with this person) tell us that

we have been able to help them ________________
(attention-getting benefit statement).

Step 4. Call for action

> "I'll be available to come to see you on ____________
> or ______________ . My number is ____________
> and I'll be available for a return call from __________
> to _________________. If I don't hear from you by
> ____________ (one week or sooner) then I'll call you
> again. Thanks in advance for your interest."

Many times the person will not call back, but because we have foreseen this event and told the person that we'll call them, we maintain the initiative (MTI) and apply gentle persistence. Therefore we call back in a week and review the previous week's call. Making another benefit statement, we say,

> "As I mentioned last week, my number is _________
> and I'll be available for a return call from _________
> to ________. If I don't hear from you by ________
> (one week or sooner), then I'll call you again. Thanks in
> advance for your interest."

If the person does not call back, we call back in a week, and review the previous two week's calls. Make another benefit statement and then say:

> "As I mentioned last week and the previous week, my
> number is _________________ and I'll be available
> for a return call from ___________ to __________.
> If I don't hear from you I'll presume that you are
> either too busy to speak right now or that you are not

interested right now. I'll make a note to try you again in _______ months."

Repeat the four steps in the number of months promised.

THE IN-PERSON APPROACH TO APPOINTMENT SETTING

Many salespeople find that the in-person approach to appointment setting can be very helpful in identifying key prospects. The problem is that many salespeople don't know how to make an in-person call or they don't have the proper attitude. In-person calls are inefficient — that is to say, one never knows if the person is going to be in and what type of response the salesperson is going to receive.

Yet the in-person call can yield much information that is not available over the phone — such as how busy the office is, numbers and types of cars in the parking lot, design and layout of the prospect's place of business, products and services displayed and so on. Plus, when you are willing to make a physical appearance, risking the ultimate face-to-face rejection, and you handle yourself in a professional, nonthreatening and businesslike manner, you can often earn the respect of the company and person you are calling on.

To demonstrate the power of in-person calls, when I started my consulting business I decided to offer a public seminar called "Building a Winning Sales Team — How to Find, Manage and Motivate Top Salespeople." To promote it, I walked from door to door in a five-square block of my office, which encompassed some 500 businesses. In addition to filling my seminar with this approach, I also met ten other people who, although they did not attend my seminar, were highly qualified and interested prospects. Four of those ten became clients within six months. So in-person calls are good for prospecting and appointment setting.

Adjust your attitude

Before we enter the door, we need to be mentally ready. Remember that our purpose is not to sell, but to listen and gather information.

- Smile.
- Have good eye contact.
- Be enthusiastic.
- Have a friendly and businesslike manner.
- Be sure to be well groomed.
- Have a dry, firm and clean handshake.
- Be sensitive to the surroundings.
- Don't interrupt busy receptionists.
- Be courteous.

What to take

You don't need to carry much for these calls but be sure to have:

- Business cards
- 3 x 5 or 4 x 6 inch cards to take notes
- Pocket calendar to book appointments

Don't take anything else. We don't want to give the impression that we've come to camp out on their doorstep and tell the entire story of our company.

A MODEL IN-PERSON APPOINTMENT SETTING CALL

To the secretary/receptionist:

> "Good morning (afternoon) _______________! My name is _______________ with _________________ (company name), a _____________________ (brief description of our business).

Hand the person your card. If you have been referred to this company, mention the referrer name now.

> "The reason I've stopped in today is to visit with the _____________ (aim high, use decision maker titles). Can you tell him/her I'm here?"

If the person isn't in:

> "That's okay. I can call back. In the meantime, do you happen to have one of his/her business cards handy? Thank you. Here's one of my cards. Please let _____________ know that I stopped in and will be calling again. By the way, what's your name?"

If the person is busy, on the phone, in a meeting, does not see people without an appointment, etc.:

> "I understand. Could you do me a favor and just take my card back to him/her and tell them that I am here and would like just a few minutes to introduce myself in person. Thanks."

If no, then proceed as above as if they're not in. If the person is in, try not to meet with the person in the lobby if at all possible. Perhaps there is a sitting area or small conference room, or maybe you can be invited into to the person's office. Don't run back to the car for samples as this visit is only an attempt to learn more about the prospect and their needs. Have a brief company overview/capabilities presentation that can be made in two minutes. Have a warm smile, good eye contact and a dry and firm handshake when the person comes out to greet you.

> "Good morning (afternoon) ________________!
> My name is _________ with__________ (company name), a ______________ (brief description of our business). Thank you for the chance to meet. The reason I stopped in today was to introduce myself and my company and find out when I might be able to visit with you for _______ (time commitment) to see if you might be able to benefit from some of the programs that our clients (drop names if appropriate) believe have been of use to them. (Have some general benefit statements handy if the person asks for examples.) Is now a convenient time or should we schedule a meeting at another time?"

If the person agrees to meet right then, move into a questioning-listening, fact-finding, rapport-building mode, which is discussed in detail in later chapters.

SAYING THANK YOU

Whether the appointment-setting call is in-person or on the phone, I always send a handwritten thank you note to anyone who was kind enough to speak with me. I can think of dozens of people who said that one of the reasons they decided to do business with me was because I sent a thank you note. Nobody seems to do it anymore, so the salesperson who says thank you really stands out. I keep it simple and always handwrite them.

If you promised specific information, it would then be appropriate to send a typed letter with the appropriate requested information.

Sample thank you message

> "Thank you for sharing your time with me today. I enjoyed talking to you and appreciated the opportunity.

I look forward to being of service to you in the future. Thanks again for your time."

FOLLOWING UP THE APPOINTMENT-SETTING CALL

Prioritize the contacts. Based on our goals and sales plans, we need to make sure that the highest priorities (those prospects with a large or immediate need) are contacted right away. An A, B, C approach will work best. "A" prospects have immediate and large potential and should be about 10% of your contacts. "B" prospects have medium potential and short to medium term needs and should be about 20% of the contacts. The balance (70%) will have either low or no potential or immediacy and will be "C" prospects.

Send every qualified A or B prospect, those where you talked to or met the decision maker, a handwritten thank you note. Keep it simple. Use half sheets of paper (5.5 x 8 inches) or blank cards that say thank you on the cover.

If you did not get the name of the secretary, administrative assistant or receptionist, call back and obtain that information now.

Within forty-eight hours, follow up with all decision makers you didn't meet. The card that was left behind has a life of about two days. The person will keep it about that long if there is some interest. After that time, a phone call will be just as effective as a cold call.

FOLLOW UP. FOLLOW UP. FOLLOW UP. Most client relationships are made after the fifth, sixth and seventh call. Eighty percent of salespeople give up after one call, 90% after two calls and 95% give up after three calls. Only 5% make the fourth, fifth and subsequent calls. BE ONE OF THE FIVE PERCENTERS!

ACTION PLAN FOR STEP THREE

Action 1. Write your thirty-second opening.

Introduction Planner

Good morning (good afternoon) Mr. (Mrs./Ms.) ___________. My name is _________________. I am with _________ (Company Name), a ________________ (brief description of your business).

____

____

____

____

____

____

____

____

____

____

____

Action 2. Write your initial benefit statements.

Benefits Planner

Now I don't know if I can be of service to you or not. The reason that I'm calling you today is because we've been able to help our clients...

and I'd like the opportunity to begin a dialogue with you to discuss ways that you may benefit from a similar relationship with our firm.

Action 3. Write down anticipated initial reflex resistances and your planned responses.

Initial Resistance and Responses Planner

I can appreciate that.
I understand how you feel.
I see your point.
I hear what you're saying.

Resistance	**Response**

The Fourth Step — Ask Questions and Listen

Once the appointment is set in Step Three, our excitement builds. We have a prospect, we know who the decision maker is, and we have an appointment with that person. Step Four, Ask Questions and Listen, is our opportunity to begin a conversation with our prospect. But this is another point in the selling process where many salespeople go wrong. Because of our excitement, and because we are most comfortable speaking about what we know, we may start telling our story too soon. Remember, people buy from those they like and trust. Our potential clients are looking for a relationship with a salesperson who is empathetic, who listens attentively and who makes them feel like an important person.

We need to resist the temptation to begin the appointment by telling our story and describing our solutions. We'll have a chance to do that later, after the prospect has had their chance to tell us about themselves, their company and their needs. We will find that if we spend the time to ask the right questions, we'll find out what people really need and want. We are best served by probing for information about the decision maker's goals, the company, the current situation, unmet needs and the like. We do this by active questioning and attentive listening.

THE FIVE-MINUTE INTRODUCTION

In some circumstances, a prospect wants to know something about us before he/she will begin to open up. In these cases, the prospect is wondering just who we are and why we think we have the right to be there asking questions and assuming solutions.

When I called on the president of a large, family-owned office products company, I began to ask questions only to learn that this person wanted first to know quite a bit about me. Each time I started to move the conversation to his needs and situation, he led the conversation back to me. Eventually, after I told him quite a bit about my background, my company and my programs, we began to move to a questioning and listening mode with me asking the questions and listening to his answers.

When you encounter this type of person, it is helpful to have a five-minute introduction prepared to explain who you are and what you stand for. This establishes in the mind of the prospect our proper intentions and that our company, products and services can meet the prospect's requirements. This short background discussion should address the following questions, which the prospect is likely to have:

- Who is this person?
- Who is this company?
- Why are they here today?
- What can they do for me?
- How long will this take?

You might start off by saying,

> "Thank you for the chance to meet with you today. You're probably wondering just who I am, what my company does, why it is important to you and what we're going to talk about. My goal today is to briefly share what my company does and my background, then spend the

majority of our time getting to know more about you, your company, your needs and how we might be of service to you. Okay?"

Share your five-minute introduction and then bridge to a questioning and listening format.

THE ART OF ASKING QUESTIONS

As I've said, people buy from people they like and trust. The best way to create this feeling is to let the prospect do most of the talking. Most people enjoy talking about themselves. All we have to do is ask the questions and then listen. It's pretty simple, but it's not easy. Some salespeople listen just briefly before formulating their sales presentation instead of using this opportunity to gather even more information.

THE BEST CONVERSATIONALIST OF OUR TIME

It has said that Dale Carnegie, the author of the world-famous, excellent book *How to Win Friends and Influence People*, was the most eloquent conversationalist of his time. He was so focused on listening that when he met someone at a business or social event he would launch into extensive open-ended questioning, encouraging the person to speak by saying things like, "Really?" "Oh?" "Is that so?" "Tell me more about...." "That's fascinating."

Carnegie would allow the other person to tell his or her story, and through his questioning, most of it innocent and simple, the other person would develop huge feelings of respect and rapport with him. Invariably, at the end of a conversation, the speaker would move on to another conversation and remark about how wonderful a conversationalist Mr. Carnegie was!

Amazing, considering that Carnegie probably said fewer than fifty words the whole time.

EARS, EYES AND MOUTH MATH

Another way of looking at this is by drawing a face with ears, eyes and a mouth.

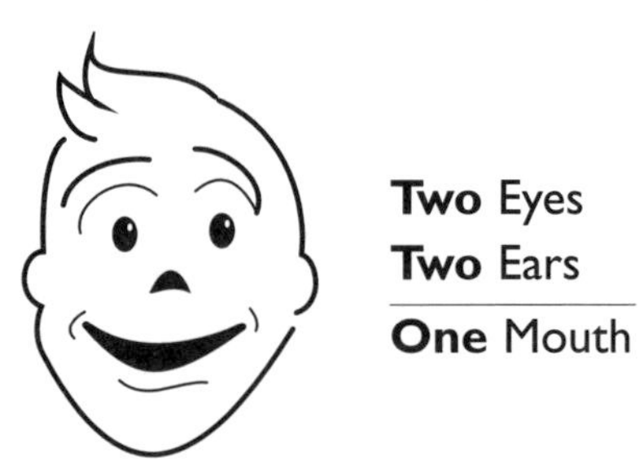

We're all given two ears, two eyes and one mouth, and we ought to use them in that ratio. We must listen and look twice as much as we talk! This runs contrary to what we have been conditioned to think about salespeople. We all have the old image of the outspoken, outgoing, glib, life of the party, backslapping, handshaking sales "pro." This is not what the professional business person or sophisticated consumer is looking for. They want someone who is a good listener and someone who is responsive to their needs. So ask questions and listen! Act as though your prospects have a big sign around their necks that says MMFI — Make Me Feel Important.

OPEN-ENDED VS. CLOSED QUESTIONS

There are two types of questions — open ended and closed. Open-ended questions encourage the other person to talk and give longer answers. These are effective for getting conversations moving. Closed questions demand one word answers (yes, no, fifteen, sometimes, maybe, etc.) and restrict conversations. They are good for pinning down information on a specific point and as transition questions that change the direction of a conversation by closing down the conversation at hand. Some people will feel like they are being interrogated when they are asked a series of mostly closed questions. Here are some examples of open-ended and closed questions.

OPEN	CLOSED
Who?	Do you?
What?	Are you?
Why?	Will you?
When?	How many?
How?	
Tell me about. . .	

THE FOUR QUESTIONS THAT CREATE TRUST AND RAPPORT

When I begin an interview with a prospect, I take out a clean sheet of paper and write four key words — NOW, BEST, LEAST and NEW — along the left margin, leaving three inches between words to write down the responses and key points that I hear. These four words represent the four categories of questions I will ask during Step Four. All of the categories are good for information gathering. The order I follow allows me to find out increasingly relevant information.

A caution: When we ask questions in these categories in a friendly, warm, businesslike and open manner, the prospect is typically going to open up to us. The way to ruin this rapport is to leap in and respond with an answer or a solution. For example, if the prospect says, "I really like the fact that product ABC comes in blue," and then we say, "My company carries ten styles of blue!" the prospect will immediately clam up and think that every time they tell us something we're going to go one better than their current situation. The best response to "I really like the fact that product ABC comes in blue," is to say, "Oh really? Is that sky blue or royal blue?" Or, "What do you like about that blue?"

In other words, use one statement as an opportunity to ask another question. If we using the four question categories in sequence, the prospect will realize that we are there to listen and to learn more about the prospect's situation and needs. The prospect will find that he or she likes and trusts us and think it's refreshing that we're not trying to sell them something. An old saying is as true today as it was fifty years ago is: *People love to buy and hate to be sold.*

Here are the four categories of questions that will help us really get to know the prospect's unmet needs, fulfilled needs, likes, dislikes and opportunities for us to be of service. I usually have four or five questions prepared for each category.

What do you have now?

This establishes the prospect's current situation. Examples of questions include:

- Quality
- Quantity
- Vendor
- Style
- Price point
- Length and depth of relationship

What do you like best about it?

This determines why they bought before and what they may want in a new option. In addition to those mentioned above, examples of questions include:

- Service
- Delivery
- Policies
- Selection
- Relationship

What do you like least about it?

This is an inoffensive way to ask what they don't like and probe for unmet needs. This sequence of questions is asked now and not in the beginning of our questions because prospects have to warm up to revealing dislikes and unhappiness with a current situation. If we led with a question asking what the prospect disliked, we might be told that everything is just fine. A bridge to this sequence of questions is:

> "No product, service, vendor or situation is perfect. What do you like least about _______?"

What would you want in a new one?

This tells us what we'll need to do to earn the right to the business. These questions help us discover the key criteria that will enable us to win or compete for this business. It is the last sequence and the opening statement is usually:

> "If you were to consider any changes (or improvements, enhancements), what would they be?" Or, "What might a company like ours do to be able to compete for (or win) your business?"

LISTENING SKILLS

Now that we've learned to ask the right questions, we had better be good at listening to the answers. It's not as easy as one might think. It's a fact that we can listen four times faster than people can talk. If the average person speaks 150 words per minute, then we can listen at the rate of 600 words per minute.

Compounding this difference is that we can listen to our "self-talk" as well as what the other person is saying and still be thinking about our surroundings, what we had for lunch, what we're going to do after work and when the dry cleaning will be ready. It is no wonder that sometimes we miss parts of the conversation. We are busy jumping ahead of the prospect, formulating answers or even planning our weekend or the rest of our lives.

So, what is listening? It is the receiver receiving information sent by the sender. This sounds easy in principle but is more difficult in practice.

OBSTACLES TO LISTENING

There are many obstacles to excellent listening. Here are just a few.

Distractions. Many people tend to live in the past or future and spend way too little time in the present. This causes us to be easily distracted and limits the effectiveness of our questioning process. Additionally, phones ring, people interrupt and the surrounding environment may be stimulating, cluttered, amazing, dirty and the like. Focusing on what the other person is saying and actively giving listening feedback such as nodding, smiling and taking notes are ways to overcome distractions.

Wandering mind. Closely related to distractions, our own wandering mind can be an obstacle to listening. We may find ourselves thinking about things totally unrelated to the task at hand. Again, active listening will prove helpful in such circumstances.

Preconceived opinions. After we have been exposed to certain sets of circumstances and types of prospects and their needs, we can have a tendency to hold onto preconceived notions. (The last person who had an office on the third floor, who wore a red tie and who had the name Arnie was rude to me, and I bet this prospect will be just the same!) The solution? Leave all of our preconceived notions at the door or in our car. There is no room for them in the sales profession.

Prejudices, appearances and accents. Sometimes we prejudge people based on their differences to us. People who talk faster or slower than us, people from a different part of the country or world, people whose dress or customs differ from ours can all present chances for missed communication and obstacles to listening. The solution is to adapt our listening to the pace, tone and style of the other person and recognize rather than resist the wide variety of cultures and customs that we are likely to be exposed to in our selling career.

WHY WE SHOULD LISTEN

It seems rather obvious why we should practice good listening skills. People buy from people they like and trust, and the best way to have someone like and trust us is to let them do most of the talking. Active listening on our part will ensure that the prospect recognizes that we are listening and paying attention. Our attentive listening is also part of a questioning approach that helps the prospect better understand their own needs, which they will appreciate, while our sequence of question categories helps us hear and understand what they are saying. Good listening is more persuasive than talking and it shows that we really care. It is a surefire technique to building trust and rapport.

HOW TO LISTEN EFFECTIVELY

- **Prepare.** Know the sequence of questions that you're going to ask and know which direction you're going with the prospect.

- **Focus.** It's been said that we can lead people anywhere we want as long as we know what questions to ask and what to do with the answers we receive.

- **Listen actively.** Give good feedback, smile, nod, take notes, repeat what the other person has said in your own words.

- **Listen selectively.** Overcome obstacles to listening and look for overall themes and ideas as they develop.

- **Reinforce relevant areas.** Ask additional questions to confirm what the prospect has said in light of how the statement might lead to solving the prospect's problems.

? ACTION PLAN FOR STEP FOUR

The best salespeople are those who are best at asking the right questions and hearing the answers. If we know what to ask and in what order, we can focus our attention on the feelings, thoughts, responses and emotions of the prospect.

Action 1. Write a five-minute overview: who you are, who your company is and what you provide to what types of people and companies.

Overview Planner

My special expertise/training/education and the accompanying benefits:

____

____

____

My company is a good place to do business because of:

____

____

____

Our clients receive the following features, benefits, services, ideas, products and support:

____

____

____

____

Action 2. Write your NOW, BEST, LEAST and NEW questions.

Questioning Planner

1. What do you have now?

2. What do you like best about it?

3. What do you like least about it?

4. What would you want in a new one?

The Fifth Step – Present the Solution

Step Four gives us extensive information about our prospects and their needs. Now we're ready to move onto Step Five, Present the Solution. We've gathered all the pertinent information from the prospect, and we're ready begin to tell our story. Now is the time to tell the prospect about the many years we've been in business and why that's important to him or her. Now is the right moment to show a list of satisfied clients, a testimonial letter or a brochure about our company. And, finally, now is the time to sell our product and services.

Bridging from Step Four to Step Five

At times, we might find ourselves in our initial appointment, which we planned in Step Four, but feeling like it's a situation in which it would be appropriate to begin presenting. Other times we just want to make a favorable impression on the prospect before coming back with a formal quote or proposal. In either case, we need to make a smooth transition from the questioning and listening phase to the presenting phase. Here is one way to accomplish that.

> "Thanks again for the chance to visit (meet) with you (today). My major reason for wanting to get together with you, of course, was to find out more

> about you and your needs, and you've done a great job of sharing that information with me. Now you're probably wondering who I am and why I even feel that I would be qualified to work with you to accomplish your objectives in this situation. So I'd like to share some specific ideas with you based on what you've told me. First permit me to spend just a few minutes sharing some information about (company name) and me, and then we'll spend the majority of our time today exploring your situation and potential solutions. All right?"

As mentioned earlier, sometimes this introduction of who you are and why you will earn the right to ask for their business is done earlier in the process, when you are working with someone who needs to know that you are competent and appropriate to talk with before they share their agenda.

DEVELOPING DYNAMIC PRESENTATIONS

It's time to tell our story, deliver solutions based on what our prospect has shared with us and create the exciting climate that will encourage the prospect to take ownership of what we have to offer. Sometimes the little things mean so much, so it is critically important to be organized: have neat and professional materials, samples and paperwork; make sure support materials are handy and appropriate; and so on. The potential client will be judging our ability to deliver on our promises by the way we present ourselves now. If we are incomplete, sloppy or disorganized during any part of the sales process (especially when we present), he or she will infer that our company is incomplete, sloppy and disorganized.

Because people buy for their reasons, not ours, the prospect wants to know *what's in it for me?* People buy benefits, the elements that make a product or service important to them. If they can say, So what? to one of our statements, then we have not demonstrated a benefit. Instead, we've probably merely described a product feature.

Tailoring our presentation to the individual or group we are meeting with will help us identify benefits. This is not to imply that we use a canned presentation, but rather that we remember to apply the ECHO principle — each call (or contact) has an objective. We may want to start in a general manner, explaining our full-service approach to the business, and then focus specifically in the areas of most benefit to the prospect.

WHAT THE CUSTOMER WANTS FROM US

As we think about the general and specific points to cover during a presentation, we ought to think about what is important to the prospect. People are looking for a company and salesperson who can be relied upon in the following areas:

- Product offerings
- Selection
- Depth
- Breadth
- Product knowledge
- Market knowledge
- Quality
- Service
- Value
- Support
- Technical expertise
- Timeliness
- Delivery
- Price Level
- Reliability
- Consistency
- Peace of mind
- Security

- Warranties
- Guarantees
- Image

Another way of considering what people need is to look at the results of a survey conducted in a major U.S. city. The study asked people to respond to the following question: "Describe the one attribute that an ideal business partner who would be selected as your provider of choice must have." Here's the result.

ATTRIBUTE	PERCENTAGE
Sales organization to be there when needed	91%
Return phone calls promptly	83%
On time performance	70%
Be honest	61%
Lowest prices	11%

As you can see, you and your company don't have to be rocket scientists with incomparable technology to be successful. Simple common sense, courtesy, honesty and a willingness to be there and on time will win the day most of the time. So it would be a good idea to demonstrate how you and your company propose to meet these needs.

USING COMPETITIVE EDGE TO DELIVER

Our competitive edge is defining how we are uniquely qualified to deliver the benefits that our clients and prospects are seeking. Our competitive edge is the list of attributes that differentiates us from our competition and articulates the distinct advantage of doing business with us. When these attributes are important to our prospects, we've made it very easy for them decide to work with us. That's key — making our competitive edge real to the customer in terms of benefits received.

How do we stand out? In any sales endeavor I've ever been engaged in, I've taken the time to look at the features and benefits of my company, its products and its services, and then written down what made my company good, better or best in each area. (Refer to the list above for ideas for your particular situation.) Then I would create a presentation book that used statistics, tables, charts, articles, industry information and customer testimonials to illustrate just how good we were.

SWOT ANALYSIS

Another way to make sure that we present ourselves in the most favorable light is to conduct a SWOT (Strengths, Weaknesses, Opportunities and Threats) Analysis of our company and our key competitors. Take separate pieces of paper for your company and for each competitor. Divide each piece into quadrants, and at the top of each quadrant list one category (strengths, weaknesses, opportunities and threats). Then list everything you can think of for each category. After doing this for your own company and your key competitors, you can focus your presentation so that it maximizes your strengths, minimizes your weaknesses, presents the best opportunities for you and protects you from threats to your standing.

WII-FM?

WII-FM stands for "What's in it for me?" and is from the prospect's perspective. If the prospect can say, "So what?" or cannot see a real benefit, then WII-FM does not really exist. For example, it is not a benefit statement for the prospect when we say that we've been in business for fifteen years or have 112 employees. There might be a reason why this is important for the prospect, but I haven't stated it as such.

A better way to say it would be, "Because we've been in business for fifteen years, we've developed quite a body of knowledge in working effectively with clients like you (we know your needs and how to respond). And with 112 people to serve you, you are likely to get the responsiveness you want when you call us or when we call you." The prospect cannot say so what to that.

FEATURES VS. BENEFITS

Once we have identified our competitive edge(s), we need to make them come to life in the minds of our prospects and clients. We do that by remembering to always communicate in terms of customer benefits, matching the features of our competitive edges to the corresponding benefits. Let's use the example of an everyday item, a clothes pin.

FEATURES (What is it or does)	CORRESPONDING BENEFITS (Why it is important)
Polished hardwood	Will not damage clothes because of splintering or discoloration
Ridges/grippers	Clothes stay on the line, so stay clean; saves money
Galvanized steel spring	No rust spots on clothing; save money on spot remover
Heavy gauge steel	Lasts a long time; good value for the money
Resealable bag with hook	Keeps clothes pins organized and available on the line; saves time

THE FOUR-PART PRESENTATION

After we have done our competitive edge analysis, we'll have a lot of information to share during any given presentation. We will ultimately be measured by our prospects based on their perceptions of us as providing the best possible solution to their problems and needs. There are four specific parts that should be in every presentation we make. Some of these will be shared early on in the relationship and some will be presented as a formal proposal. The important point to remember is that the prospect will have to be convinced in all four parts of our presentation in order for a business relationship to develop.

Part 1. Tell our personal story.
This part shows that we are competent, have the right intentions and are the appropriate person to do business with.

Part 2. Tell the company story.
This part demonstrates our company ability, skills and knowledge to do the business right.

Part 3. Present our services.
This shows what our competitive edge is.

Part 4. Present our solution(s), product(s), service(s).
This part solves the problem, fills a need, helps the prospect or client achieve what they want.

PRESENTATION MANUALS

It's best to engage as many senses as we can, through presentation books, handouts and support material. Some people are visual in their approach to buying, and if we only use our mouths during our presentation to them, we'll be less effective. Included in the presentation manual are sources and documentation of our credibility — catalogs, testimonial letters, awards, work samples, pictures of our company and employees, product information, technical specifications and the like. The list is limited only by our imagination. For the best flow, organize the presentation book to follow the four-part presentation outlined above.

ANTICIPATING OBJECTIONS

Our company, service(s) and products are not always going to be the perfect solution to every situation. Sometimes we are not going to be the best choice and that is okay. Yet there will be many times when our solution is just as valid as one of our competitors, and what will differentiate us from them will be how well we present our solution and how well we anticipate and overcome objections to our offering. The best way to do this is to plan for as many possibilities as we can, preparing answers in advance and even going so far as to present the potential objection ourselves during our presentation and then countering it with our answer.

POTENTIAL OBJECTION	ANSWER
Larger competitor	Personal attention from a smaller company
Previous bad experience	Changes made to increase service level
Loyalty to a competitor	Acceptance and desire for secondary position

TESTIMONIAL LETTERS

Using testimonial letters is such an important selling tool. The salesperson who learns this will reap the dividends of increased business. Unfortunately, most people are busy and so generally won't have the time or take the initiative to write them for us. We have to ask for them and even draft the letters ourselves based on the service we've provided. Over the years, I've asked for and received more than one hundred testimonial letters. They've been great for me for two reasons. First, my prospects read wonderful things about me, written by satisfied clients. Second, many times my prospects recognize the company or person who signed the testimonial. When this happens for you, it immediately increases your value and credibility in the mind of your prospect. Testimonial letters:

- Give us credibility with people who don't know us well.
- Make us unique in the eyes of the prospect.
- Enable us to tell stories of people in similar situations who we've helped in the past.
- Give the message that we are professional and do a good job.

You can collect testimonial letters by:

- Asking for a testimonial letter as a favor.
- Explaining that a testimonial letter will help you differentiate yourself from other salespeople.
- Offer to write the general points for them.
- Give them some examples to look at.

SATISFIED CUSTOMER LISTS

If you are shy about asking for a testimonial letter, at least ask your clients for permission to list their names as a satisfied clients. Use the format on the next page and print it out on your letterhead. The more names on the page, the better you look. I can place forty on a page, single spaced, in twelve-point type.

Satisfied Customers of Warren Wechsler
Total Selling Systems

NAME/TITLE/COMPANY	PHONE	SITUATION
Mr. Jon Brown, President Amazing Delivery, Inc.	888-8000	Increased sales 20%
Ms. Jill Green, CEO Best Flowers, Inc.	989-9988	Trained two new hires
Mr. Bob Black Great Properties	777-6543	Keynote speech to 250 Realtors

! ACTION PLAN FOR STEP FIVE

Action 1. Write the four-part presentation.

Presentation Planner

1. My personal story (competency and credibility):

____

____

____

2. My company's story (values, mission, competitive edge):

____

____

____

3. Our services (benefits to the prospect):

____

____

____

4. Our solution(s)/product(s) (the reason to buy):

____

____

____

____

Action 2: Write down the objections most likely to be encountered and the appropriate responses.

Objections Planner

Objection	Response

Action 3. Create a presentation manual.

Presentation Manual Planner

My presentation manual will contain the following:

The Sixth Step — Ask for the Commitment

We've successfully worked our way up the selling pyramid and are now ready for Step Six, Ask for the Commitment. Most traditional sales programs call this step "closing the sale." But that perspective causes many salespeople to become overly aggressive. The fact is, we cannot really close the sale. We can't twist the arm of the prospect and demand that they "sign here!"

We can, and must, however, *ask* for the commitment. And by asking the right obligating questions at the right times, and knowing how to work with various responses, we will be excellent at opening new accounts, developing relationships and turning prospects into clients.

One of my early mentors in sales told me that I was more like a professional "visitor" than a professional salesperson. I was effective at finding the prospect and finding the decision maker. I had a healthy number of appointments per week. I asked good questions, listened well and presented myself, my company and my products in an enthusiastic and effective manner. Yet, at the end of the sales process, I either waited for the prospect to ask me how to buy or left without the order.

Upon examination, it became clear that I was not asking for the sale. Like many sale people, I hadn't learned to ask obligating questions and maintain the initiative. I had learned to follow the first five steps, but I didn't yet realized that, by doing so, I earned the right to ask the prospect to commit to me. I started asking people direct, nonmanipulative questions about finalizing the sales process. My sales and income literally quadrupled overnight! I went from being a moderately successful salesperson to the top salesperson in my company.

DEVELOPING A COMMITMENT MENTALITY

To become a professional and a complete salesperson, we need to develop a commitment mentality — and not just for the end of the sales process. A commitment mentality entails knowing when and how to ask obligating questions. Although the major impact for us will come at the end of sales process, we utilize opportunities all along the way to manifest this attitude.

OUR COMMITMENT OPPORTUNITIES

We have several opportunities during the sales process for asking obligating questions for appropriate commitment from the prospect.

- Commitment for information on an initial call.
- Commitment for decision-making criteria.
- Commitment for an appointment.
- Commitment for a quote or proposal.
- Commitment for a second appointment.
- Commitment for order, sale or relationship.

THE PHILOSOPHY OF COMMITMENT

Many sales-training books, tapes and seminars are filled with manipulative, contrived and gimmicky techniques. There is the "Ben Franklin" close, the "let me think it over" close, the "reduce to the ridiculous" close, the "puppy dog" close, the "alternative of choice" close, the "my dear old mother told me" close, the "silence is consent" close and the "final objection" close, to name just a few. I know every one of them because I memorized them as I studied early sales techniques. *I never use any of them.* They make me feel unprofessional.

Today consumers are much more sophisticated than in the past. Questions like "Would you like to take delivery next week or right away?" or "Would you like to go with the full carton or a half carton?" will not work with most people. Sure, we might be occasionally successful using a contrived close, but not because we are strong closers. These commitment techniques work only when the decision to move forward has *already* been made in the mind of the prospect.

Fortunately, there is a better way to move the sales process along easily and naturally. It's not high pressure or manipulative. It doesn't mean that salespeople don't suggest solutions, encourage decisions or maintain control of the commitment phase of the sales process. The better approach to getting a commitment is incorporating the philosophy of commitment into the entire selling process.

- You make it easy for the prospect to say yes by becoming an expert at applying the principles in the first five steps of the six-step selling model.

- You know when to start listening for the yes, and then move into Step Six and ask an obligating question.

Making it easy for the prospect to say yes begins the first time the salesperson and the prospect talk. When we answer the prospect's questions properly and listen attentively, we make it easier for the prospect to like and trust us, which makes it easier for him/her to say yes. Other ways during the sales process to make it easy are:

- Knowing why you called the prospect, why the prospect agreed to an appointment, why the prospect wanted you to make your presentation and how the prospect will make the buying decision.

- Anticipating potential resistance and reasons why the process will not end with a commitment and having convincing answers to counter the objections.

- Listening carefully, probing for needs, making the prospect feel that his/her feelings, point of view and situation are important.

- Preparing a dynamic and personalized presentation that solves the prospect's immediate and long-term problems, creating the perfect buying environment.

Knowing when to start listening for the yes is a discipline that can be developed. Prospects with some reluctance to go forward will let us know. If not, then they will simply say yes. That's what commitment is all about. The overture is made by the salesperson and the rest is up to the prospect. The salesperson has simply helped the prospect make the right decision for both parties, and most likely, the decision the prospect wanted to make all along.

The timing on this point is very important. In some situations, the prospect won't make a decision during the presentation and physical visit with the salesperson. If this is the case, it is vitally important to ask for the commitment time and sequence so that we can maintain the initiative and know when to ask the obligating question. Sometimes persistence and a willingness to gain agreement at each point in the process will ensure that, when it's the right time to place the order, we are in position to ask the right questions.

After all, if we work for the best company (say yes) and have the best products (say yes) and are the best salespeople that we can be (say yes), we owe it to our prospects to have them become involved with us!

HOW TO ASK FOR THE COMMITMENT

This final commitment phase is easy because there are only two rules to remember:

Rule #1. Ask an obligating question.

Rule #2. Be QUIET!

The sales books from the 1950s onward said rule number two was "SHUT UP!" because the first person who speaks loses. In my view, they had the rule right but the reason wrong. We practice silence after asking for the decision simply to give the prospect a chance to evaluate the offer and make a decision, not to win the round. We all go a little crazy just before we make a decision to buy something. If someone else is talking the whole time, it becomes even more difficult to come to a decision. This usually leads to indecision or statements like "I need to think about it some more," or "I'll come back later," or "Let me get back to you."

Think about your own buying experiences. Before you know you need some product or service, you're at equilibrium. Then something changes. Something breaks or a new technology becomes available. You begin to gather information, evaluate your needs and listen to a professional salesperson. The time arrives to make a decision. If it is a very important or expensive purchase, the decision may be scary. At this point, everybody tends to have internal discussions with themselves. This is called decision anxiety. You want to get the decision over, but you don't want to make the wrong decision. You feel like a yo-yo. Yes, no, yes, no…

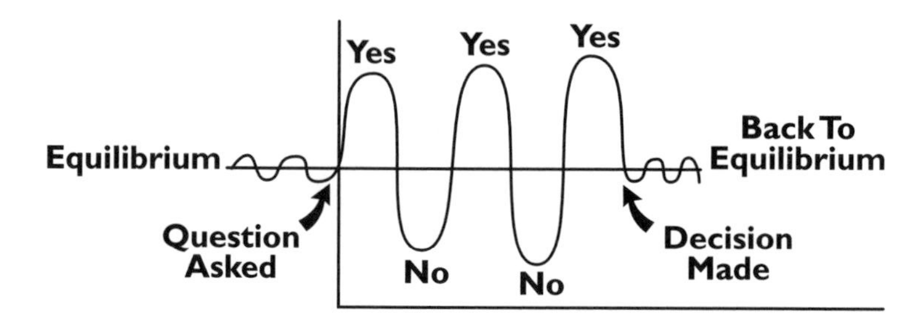

All you really want is to make the right decision, return to equilibrium and then move on to something else. Imagine what it would be like if, while going through this decision phase, someone was talking to you the entire time. It doesn't matter whether the person is talking about reasons to buy or going on and on with mindless chatter or nervous chitchat. It interferes with your completion of your internal decision-making process.

This is why it is so important for us as salespeople to follow the two rules. First, we ask an obligating question to start the prospect's internal decision-making process. Then we remain quiet so the prospect can reach a conclusion.

BEING NEUTRAL TO THE OUTCOME OF THE OBLIGATING QUESTION

In addition to developing the discipline to follow the two rules of how to ask for a commitment, we also need to learn to be neutral to the outcome. We *can* control the asking of the question. We *cannot* control the response of the prospect. If we are caught up emotionally in whether the prospect says yes or no, we won't be in a position to listen to and overcome resistance if we encounter it. Also, the prospect will feel the pressure from us and will not easily move into a buying mode.

The more prospects we move through the first five steps, the easier it will be for us to remain neutral to the outcome. We won't feel so pressured. Based on the numbers, someone will eventually say yes. We just don't know if it is going to be on this appointment or the next or the next. If our universe of people who have been through the five steps is small, we will put so much importance on each obligating question that it will be difficult to remain neutral.

There are only three possible responses to our obligating question.

1. Yes (What we love to hear.)
2. No (What we can learn to love to hear.)
3. Maybe (What we least like to hear.)

WHEN THE ANSWER IS YES

This is simple. We sincerely thank the prospect (now a client!) for the opportunity to be of service and bring out the appropriate contracts, forms and other paperwork. As we begin completing them, we reinforce the client's decision to move forward as a wise choice. This will reduce feelings of buyer's remorse, cancelled orders or potential concerns.

WHEN THE ANSWER IS NO

"No" is more complicated. We've progressed through the first five steps with this prospect and our expectation was for a yes. By saying no, the prospect has either temporarily or permanently stopped the movement toward yes. There are two potential scenarios. The prospect raises either a condition or an objection.

A *condition* is a valid reason for not moving forward and usually beyond our control. Examples of a condition are the wrong solution, no money, no need or not an appropriate solution. A condition will typically not be raised if we have done the proper qualifying in Step Two.

An *objection* is not a valid reason for stopping at no because it is usually in our control. For example, it could mean that there has been a lack of communication, the prospect needs more information or isn't convinced of the benefits yet, or we asked too soon.

We can overcome objections but not conditions. Conditions should be tested, however, to see if they can be made into objections and then overcome.

We will be much more effective in our selling careers when we know what we are likely to encounter and prepare our response in advance. The worst case for us is knowing the answer but not being able to present it when we hear the objection because we are in a state of panic or uncertainty.

In any event, we are entitled to ask why when the prospect says no. We don't get defensive. We simply and sincerely ask why the person said no. For example, "I'm surprised to hear you say that. Do you mind if I ask what it is?" Then smile and be quiet. Maybe we left something out of our presentation or the prospect misinterpreted our offer. There might be an easy opportunity to turn the no into a yes — as long as we remain calm and neutral to the outcome. In my experience, when people say no, often they are looking for more information and a reason to say yes.

Three ways to respond to no and learn why

Without arguing or becoming defensive, begin with a statement such as:

> I can appreciate that.
> I understand how you feel.
> I see what you mean.
> I hear what you are saying.

(1)
Salesperson: Do you mind if I ask what your objection is?
Prospect: No, I don't mind.

Salesperson: What is it? (Gets us more specific information.)
Prospect: (Gives specific objection.)
Salesperson: (Answers objection and asks for the commitment again.)

(2)
Salesperson: It seems as though there is some reluctance to move ahead today. What is holding you back?
Prospect: (Specific objection.)
Salesperson: (Answers objection and asks for the commitment again.)

(3)
Salesperson: I can appreciate that you have some additional concerns. What are they?
Prospect: (Specific objection.)
Salesperson: (Answers objection and asks for the commitment again.)

The dos and don'ts of effectively overcoming an objection

Don't argue.
Don't challenge the prospect's emotions.
Don't challenge the wisdom of the prospect's decision.
Don't burn bridges.

Do show empathy.
Do be a good listener.
Do attempt to get to the underlying issues.
Do suggest alternative solutions.
Do be creative.
Do remain open to ideas.
Do remain calm.
Do keep lines of communication open.

Do anticipate objections and be prepared to answer them.

OBJECTION	ANSWER
Need for different size, style	Special order it at same price
Need it sooner	Check into "rush" status
New idea or product	Offer to extend warranty or guarantee repurchase
Cash-flow difficulties	Extend terms to qualified clients

Do if appropriate raise the objection yourself and the answer it. For example:

> "Many people have thought that (objection) and I can understand how you might feel that way also. Here is what we found upon further examination (answer it)."

THE SPECIAL CASE OF PRICING OBJECTIONS

Price is rarely the reason people take their business elsewhere. It is true that most of us would closely scrutinize two offers whose prices were very different when everything else were equal. Our goal is to see if they really are equal, because it is almost always true that we get what we pay for. To test the price objection, we want the other person to talk about it so we can have the facts on the table. Most of the time the salesperson is more defensive about the price than the prospect. Use one of the following responses when confronted with, "Your price is too high!"

- "The price is too high?"
- "Too high in what respect?"
- "Just how do you mean?"
- "Too high compared to what?"

Our goal when faced with a price objection is to have the prospect explain the difference in price. Once we know what is behind the price issue, we handle it like any other objection.

(1)
Prospect: Your price is too high.
Salesperson: I can appreciate that you feel that way. Tell me, why do you feel that our price is too high?
(Uncover the reason behind their position and determine if it is a condition or an objection.)

(2)
Prospect: I can get a ________ for $2 less per unit and it's the same product.
Salesperson: If they are the same, you probably should buy the _________. Let's look at them and see if there is any value for the additional $2.
(We are positioning the relationship between price and value in the mind of the client.)

The client sees: **PRICE** Value

We see: Price **VALUE**

A commitment is created when price is perceived to be equal to value. We achieve this by remembering to develop the concept of competitive edge. We need to show how we are different, better, unique and add value in the areas of importance to the customer.

WHEN THE ANSWER IS MAYBE

Maybe is the response that can drive salespeople to distraction. Some examples of maybe are:

- I have to think it over.
- It sounds good but let me sleep on it.
- I'll get back to you.
- Let me talk it over with so and so.

Maybe is usually a result of unclear communication, a violation or omission of one of the five previous steps. Our goal is to turn maybe into something more specific. Again, we're entitled to ask why. We don't get defensive and we sincerely ask why the person isn't ready to decide one way or the other. For example:

> "I'm surprised to hear you say that because of what we've discovered and agreed on so far. I'm sure you have a good reason for saying you want to think it over. Just what about the decision do you want to think over?"

If the prospect has a hard time focusing on what it is they want to think over, sleep on, talk over and so on, we can follow up by mentioning areas that they may be thinking about:

- The offer
- The quantity
- The product
- The service
- The specifications
- Competing offering
- Delivery
- Pricing
- The warranty
- Our company
- Us

Dealing with a maybe then is handled in a similar fashion to when we hear a no. Our goal is to turn the maybe into a yes or a no and remaining neutral to the outcome. As long as a decision is made and we did the best we could to get the customer involved in our product, we're okay with either a yes or a no.

Ways to response when the prospect says maybe

(1)
Prospect: I need to think it over.
Salesperson: I understand. What do you need to think
over? Is it...
(Mention specific benefit examples based on
your conversations)

(2)
Prospect: I want to sleep on it.
Salesperson: I can appreciate that. What do you want to
sleep on. Is it...
(Again, use specific examples based on your conversations)

MAINTAINING THE INITIATIVE — REVISITED

Whether the prospect says no or maybe, if we cannot get to the commitment at this meeting, we need to remember to maintain the initiative. A simple statement like, "When should I call you back to follow up?" works well.

ARE WE BEING HIGH PRESSURE?

The techniques of asking for the commitment are not high pressure, dishonest or manipulative. Rather, they present opportunities for the prospect to come to a decision and not procrastinate. Being assertive during this commitment phase, or any other phase of the selling process, creates more respect for us in the mind of the prospect. It helps our prospects make good decisions and helps us in making profitable sales, building market share and remaining successful.

GETTING INTO THE HALL OF FAME

Remember the Hall of Fame statistic, and you'll understand that you cannot be successful with everybody. A major league baseball player has a chance to make a hit or be struck out every time he comes to bat. When a baseball player has an average of three successes out of ten (.300) that player is just about guaranteed entry into the Hall of Fame. What would happen if you applied that same statistic in your sales careers? Are you now willing to take lots more swings — that is, ask more obligating questions and successfully complete Step Six?

ACTION PLAN FOR STEP SIX

Action 1. Write some obligating questions for your business and product.

Commitment Planner

The specific questions that I will use to get the commitment are:

Action 2. Write objections you anticipate and answer them.

Response Planner

When I hear NO I will respond with the following:

When I hear MAYBE I will respond by saying the following:

Time to Take Action!

You've now worked through the six steps to excellence in selling. You know why the six steps are important, what each means and how to create your personal and unique plan for each step. What's next?

It's time to put your new knowledge to work! I've found that the salespeople who actually do something with the knowledge they have learned are the people who later report back great achievements and success. They find that the actions they take produce almost immediate results. Those positive results fire their desire to continue the activities and techniques that produced the results.

To make the most of what you've learned, take action by tracking your statistics, forecasting your success and buddying up. Here's how.

TRACK YOUR STATISTICS

The first strategy for ensuring your sales success is to set some realistic and measurable goals that can be translated into activities you can monitor. For example, maybe you decide to increase your monthly sales by 20%. To accomplish that, you would need a particular number of new clients (use the sales ratio analysis you did in Step One). You can now establish benchmarks for yourself in many areas. Track your progress by recording on a sheet with the sales statistics headings shown on page 158.

Record your daily activities as they happen. Look at the statistics and analyze your numbers weekly. Over time, you'll be able to see where you need additional focus, review or skill development. If you are reaching a lot of decision makers and setting few appointments, you're probably trying to sell your products and services, instead of an initial appointment. If you are seeing a lot of people and asking for few commitments, you'll need to remember to ask for the commitment. You'll become skilled at areas that need attention and see where your strengths are.

FORECAST YOUR SUCCESS

The second action step you can take to help you maximize the knowledge you've learned through this book is to forecast your success. This will show you how mature your sales pipeline is and how aggressive you need to be in putting more prospects into your funnel. Set up a forecasting form with the headings shown on page 160. Record your statistics daily, then once a week review them to see how many prospects are moving through the six steps and which ones are likely to become customers. As the list shrinks, more new prospects will need to be added to keep your momentum moving in a positive direction.

BUDDY UP

The third action step to take to give yourself the best opportunity for success is to "buddy up" with another salesperson and encourage each other to establish goals, measure statistics and stay on course. This is an incredibly powerful technique. There is a synergy that develops when two or more people are focused on a similar path. Napoleon Hill, author of *Think and Grow Rich*, called this the MasterMind concept. I've used the idea to increase my earnings by tens of thousands of dollars. It's easy to learn and easy to apply.

First, find a buddy. Agree to meet once a week for one hour. At the first meeting, both you and your buddy fill out in duplicate the agreement shown on page 161. (Each person is a salesperson and becomes a buddy for the other person.) At the weekly meetings, review your goals, measure your progress, and support and encourage each other.

Congratulations! You've put the concepts of *The Six Steps to Excellence in Selling* into action and you're on your way. Good selling to you!

SALES STATISTICS

Day/Date	Attempts/Dials	Contacts to Decision Makers	Appointments Set	Presentations Made	Commitments Asked For	Commitments Received

SALES FORECAST

Company	Phone	Decision Maker Name	Initial Approach Date	Appointment Date	Presentation Made	Status/Will Close

EXCELLENCE IN SELLING AGREEMENT

Purpose: To achieve sales objectives established by

____________________ and ____________________.
(Salesperson) (Buddy)

Activities:

1. _______ prospecting calls per week. Sales statistics to be tracked daily and discussed at weekly meeting.
2. _______ contacts per week. Sales statistics to be tracked daily and discussed at weekly meeting.
3. _______ appointments per week. Appointments to be written in daily planner and discussed at weekly meeting.
4. _______ new accounts to be opened per month based on above activities. Sales forecast to be updated daily and discussed at weekly meeting.
5. _______ commissions/sales to be generated per month. Goals and actual results will be reviewed at the weekly meeting.
6. Other ______________________________________

   ____

   ____.

Agreed and accepted by: (Salesperson)	Agreed and accepted by: (Buddy)
Name____________________	Name____________________
Title____________________	Title____________________
Date____________________	Date____________________

RECOMMENDED READING LIST

SELLING

Allesandra, Tony et al. *Non-Manipulative Selling.* New York: Simon and Shuster, 1987.

Bettger, Frank. *How I Raised Myself from Failure to Success in Selling.* New York: Simon and Shuster, 1949.

Carew, Jack. *You'll Never Get No for an Answer.* New York: Simon and Shuster, 1987.

Girard, Joe. *How to Sell Yourself.* New York: Warner Books, 1979.

Hanan, Mack. *Key Account Selling.* New York: AMACOM, 1989.

Hopkins, Tom. *How to Master the Art of Selling Anything.* Scottsdale, AZ: Champion Press, 1982.

Trisler, Hank. *No Bull Selling.* New York: Frederick Fell Publishers, 1983.

Wilson, Larry and Spencer Johnson. *The One Minute Salesperson.* New York: Candle Communications, 1994.

Ziglar, Zig. *Secrets of Closing the Sale.* Old Tappan, NJ: Fleming R. Revell Co., 1984.

ATTITUDE

Carnegie, Dale. *How to Win Friends and Influence People.* New York: Simon and Shuster, 1936.

Peale, Norman Vincent. *The Power of Positive Thinking.* New York: Prentice-Hall, 1952.

Schwartz, David J. *The Magic of Thinking Big.* Englewood Cliffs, NJ: Prentice-Hall, 1959.

(Continued on next page)

GOALS

Covey, Stephen R. *Seven Habits of Highly Effective People.* New York: Simon and Shuster, 1989.

Hill, Napoleon. *Think and Grow Rich.* New York: Hawthorn Books, 1937.

Leider, Richard J. *The Power of Purpose.* New York: Fawcett Gold Medal, 1985.

Maltz, Maxwell. *Psycho-Cybernetics.* Englewood Cliffs, NJ: Prentice-Hall, 1960.

TIME MANAGEMENT

Lakein, Alan. *How to Get Control of Your Time and Your Life.* New York: Signet, 1974.

ABOUT WARREN WECHSLER

Warren Wechsler is an award-winning salesperson, successful sales manager, skillful trainer and prosperous business owner. He has been actively engaged in sales- and service-driven companies for two decades. Through his own personal selling, the observation and training of other salespeople and the study of sales and marketing theory and techniques, he has identified and mastered the skills utilized by all successful sales and marketing people.

Founder and president of TOTAL SELLING SYSTEMS™, a Minneapolis-based sales training company, Mr. Wechsler devotes his full-time energies to his stated mission of helping sales, marketing and other professional people rise to their highest possible level of achievement through sales training, self-management, goal setting, strategic sales planning and other personal development programs.

He presents many of his programs in-house, such as at company sales meetings, half-day workshops, full-day seminars and strategic sales planning meetings.

In addition to his work within companies, Mr. Wechsler is often a keynote speaker at association meetings, conventions and trade shows. He a member of Network USA, Rotary International and Toastmasters International.

Mr. Wechsler is married and the proud father of two daughters. In his leisure time he enjoys long-distance running, travel and cooking.

To bring Warren Wechsler to your company, sales conference, convention or trade association gathering, contact:

TOTAL SELLING SYSTEMS
7101 York Avenue South
Edina, MN 55435
(612) 921-3388

INDEX

ORDER FORM

Please send me ______ copy (copies) of *The Six Steps to Excellence in Selling* by Warren Wechsler, at a cost of $17.95 each (includes a $3.00 shipping and handling cost.) (In Minnesota, add sales tax for a total of $18.93 per book.)

☐ Check enclosed for ______________

☐ Bill my credit card (Visa or Mastercard)

Card number ______________________________

Expiration Date ________________

Signature _____________________ Date________

Name ____

Company ____

Address ____

City ___________________ State _______ Zip ___________

☐ Yes, I would like the book(s) autographed to:

____

____

____

Mail or fax to: Better Books, 7101 York Ave. S.
Edina, MN 55435-4408, Fax (612) 921-3271